58190

Y0-GGF-082

HOUSING ASSISTANCE FOR OLDER AMERICANS

The Reagan Prescription

James P. Zais
Raymond J. Struyk
Thomas Thibodeau

Library
St. Joseph's College
Patchogue, N.Y. 11772

An Urban Institute Paperback

THE URBAN INSTITUTE PRESS · WASHINGTON, D.C.

Copyright © 1982
The Urban Institute
2100 M Street, N.W.
Washington, D.C. 20037

Printed in the United States of America

LC 82-50957
ISBN 0-87766-317-3
Please refer to URI 34300 when ordering

BOARD OF TRUSTEES
William D. Ruckelshaus
Chairman
Katharine Graham
Vice Chairman
William Gorham
President
Warren E. Buffett
Joseph A. Califano, Jr.
William T. Coleman, Jr.
John M. Deutch
Anthony Downs
John H. Filer
Joel L. Fleishman
Philip M. Hawley
Aileen C. Hernandez
Carla A. Hills
Ray L. Hunt
Robert S. McNamara
Lois D. Rice
Henry B. Schacht

LIFE TRUSTEES
Eugene G. Fubini
Vernon E. Jordan, Jr.
Edward H. Levi
Bayless A. Manning
Stanley Marcus
Arjay Miller
J. Irwin Miller
Franklin D. Murphy
Herbert E. Scarf
Charles L. Schultze
William W. Scranton
Cyrus R. Vance
James Vorenberg

THE URBAN INSTITUTE is a nonprofit policy research and educational organization established in Washington, D.C. in 1968. Its staff investigates interrelated social and economic problems of urban communities, and government policies affecting those communities and the people who live in them. The Institute disseminates significant findings of such research through the active publications program of its Press. The Institute has two goals for work in each of its research areas: to help shape thinking about societal problems and efforts to solve them, and to improve government decisions and performance by providing better information and analytic tools.

Through work that ranges from broad conceptual studies to administrative and technical assistance, Institute researchers contribute to the stock of knowledge available to public officials and to private individuals and groups concerned with formulating and implementing more efficient and effective government policy.

Conclusions or opinions expressed are those of the authors and do not necessarily reflect the views of other staff members, officers or trustees of the Institute, or of any organizations which provide financial support to the Institute.

CONTENTS

TABLES

FIGURES

FOREWORD

This report is part of the "Changing Domestic Priorities" project of The Urban Institute. This project is examining the shifts that are occurring in the nation's economic and social policies under the Reagan administration and analyzing the effects of these changes on people, places, and institutions.

As with many other aspects of economic and social policy, the Reagan administration's program for housing assistance represents a major departure from past federal prescriptions. The primary thrust of the president's program is to greatly reduce the federal government's role in providing housing assistance. To accomplish this, the administration has proposed to arrest the budgetary growth of housing assistance programs, to target the remaining assistance on those most in need, and to rely almost exclusively on direct assistance to households in existing units. The vehicle for providing the direct subsidies to households would be so-called "housing vouchers," which would be income-conditioned (with their value varying inversely with household income) and predicated on the household living in a unit meeting certain minimum standards established by program rules. The basic federal approach since 1974 had relied heavily upon subsidies to the suppliers of housing, with flexibility given to localities to determine the relative emphasis of the use of the existing housing stock or more costly new construction projects.

These policies have special implications for older Americans. The majority of the elderly own their homes. Elderly renters, however, tend to be poorer, are more likely to live in substandard units, and have little opportunity for improving their incomes. Impoverished elderly renters, most of whom reside in urban areas, might therefore be reasonably considered to be among the "truly needy" and most deserving of governmental assistance.

To analyze the implications of these new policy directions, Zais, Struyk, and Thibodeau have taken considerable advantage of data from the Experimental Housing Allowance program, which tested various forms of housing vouchers in 12 sites for nearly a decade. The experimental program provided the information needed for generating predictions about participation and benefit levels under various specific program designs. These are applied by the authors to the national elderly population through the use of a model that simulates the benefit levels that elderly participants would be receiving in 1983 under the plan proposed by the Reagan administration. These estimates are compared with benefits that would be received under the present approach. The authors show that individual elderly households that are assisted would receive a much smaller subsidy under the Reagan proposals than under the current mix of programs. At the same time, the elderly as a percentage of all households assisted would probably increase because they are more likely to qualify for payments without moving and because efforts to target assistance to households with lower incomes result in a larger proportion of elderly in the eligible population.

Some of the Reagan administration's proposals for housing assistance have already been enacted and others are still being debated. As with all the research that will be published in this series, our hope is that the analysis herein will help shape more informed public policy as the Congress and the nation react to these new policy directions.

John L. Palmer
Isabel V. Sawhill

General Editors
Changing Domestic Priorities Series

ACKNOWLEDGMENTS

We are particularly grateful to the Retirement Research Foundation for sponsoring the work reported in this book. Marilyn Hennessey at the Foundation encouraged us to analyze the proposals that the Reagan administration offered for housing policy with special emphasis on the elderly, as quickly as possible so that current legislative discussion could be enriched and to provide a lasting record of the probable impact of these types of proposals on the elderly. In addition, we appreciatively acknowledge the support of the Aetna Life and Casualty Foundation in permitting us to make final emendations to the manuscript for publication as a book.

For valuable contributions to the completion of this report, we would especially like to acknowledge the competent computer programming by Tri Hoang, Anne Bergsman, Eric Simon, and Don Manson. Harold Williams of the Department of Housing and Urban Development helped us in interpreting several data bases on housing program participants. Finally, we want to thank Sue Marshall for providing valuable comments on an earlier draft.

Chapter 1

INTRODUCTION

For more than four decades, the federal government has supported housing assistance programs designed to help low and moderate income households to buy or rent adequate housing. With few major interruptions, this system of housing programs has grown in both budgetary commitments and the number of households assisted. By the end of 1980, over a third of those assisted by renter programs were elderly, using the Department of Housing and Urban Development's (HUD) definition of elderly as those whose household head is 62 years of age or older.

The advent of the Reagan administration in January of 1981 may have marked a clear turning point in federal housing policy, as in many other areas of domestic policy. The particulars of the change are still in process and are subject to further debate within the administration and in the Congress. But in its early months the administration has made it clear that there is to be a drastic cutback in the overall level of assistance. During previous administrations, the key statistic was the number of additional households to be assisted in the next fiscal year. The housing assistance policy proposed during the early Reagan administration is that there will be no increase in the number of households receiving household subsidies.

Beyond the overall level of assistance, it has also become clear that, with few exceptions, this administration wants to rely on the existing housing stock to provide the actual dwelling units, as opposed to constructing new housing projects. Since the Second World War, the federal government has employed three major forms of assistance: public housing, subsidized newly constructed units (built by the private sector), and assistance to households living in existing units in the private market. The oldest of these, public housing, dates back to 1937. The youngest is a family of "leased housing" programs that began with the Section 23 program in 1965 and currently takes the form of the "Section 8 Existing" program. Perhaps because of its belief in the workings of the private market, but most certainly because of the lower per household costs of approaches that utilize "existing" housing units, the administration is pursuing a policy of heavy, if not exclusive, reliance on a program of this type.

Indeed, the major administration initiative is called the "Modified Section 8 Certificate." Others have labeled this approach "housing vouchers," "housing allowances," or "consumer assistance grants," but whatever the label, the basic idea is similar. Housing assistance payments are given to households (or to landlords on behalf of households) on the basis of income-eligibility, provided the household lives in a dwelling which meets certain program standards. The standards involve minimal levels of physical condition, as well as sufficient size to meet the needs of the household assisted. The actual choice of the unit, however, is up to the household. Hence, the "voucher" approach is associated with households, and is not tied to units in the way that programs developing new housing or substantially rehabilitating existing housing are.

As we shall see in this report, the administration's voucher proposal goes the greatest distance in providing consumer freedom of choice, compared with other "existing" housing programs used so far by the federal government. With few constraints, households can live where they want and pay the amount of rent they choose. From the household's standpoint, these program features appear attractive. On the other hand, benefit levels are dramatically lower in the new proposal than in programs it will replace. This is a feature that will cause some would-be participants to shun the program and, indeed, may make the new program essentially unworkable.

In this report we will look at how elderly-headed households are likely to fare under this approach and how other changes that were enacted in 1981 as well as those proposed in the administration's FY 1983 budget, will affect the participation of elderly persons in housing assistance programs.

This examination is of interest not only because it provides insights into the specific proposals of the Reagan administration, which may or may not be accepted by the Congress. Far more importantly, the analysis informs us about the consequences for elderly Americans of general types of change in U.S. housing policy. In a very real sense, the Reagan proposals have provided us an opportunity to document the impacts of a variety of changes, and the utility of this information will continue for several years as a basis for evaluating other proposals that are advanced by the administration and the Congress.

There are a number of good reasons for singling out the elderly for such special analysis. From a societal point of view, there has been a growing recognition in the past few years that the most humane and cost-effective public policies toward the elderly are those which assist as many older people as possible to remain in their communities, rather than be institutionalized. Almost every contemporary issue relating to the elderly—mandatory retirement age, pension and Social Security reform, national health insurance—brings with it questions about the extent to which independent living by the elderly will be enhanced or deterred. Housing policy is no exception. Housing assistance is a key element in sustaining many of the roughly one-million elderly renters who receive such help in the community, although we do not know the precise effect.

The hallmark of the relation between the elderly and their housing is that housing needs change as people age. Incomes are likely to be reduced, a spouse may die, a son or daughter may leave home or return, and physical and health problems may become more restricting. These factors relate directly to the ability of older people to pay for or maintain their current dwellings, or to search for and locate alternative units in the community.

Unlike their younger counterparts, the elderly most often do not approach housing as an investment good per se, although the bequest motive is important. Rather, they see housing more simply as a place to live. Their psychological attachment to their dwellings is probably greater than it is for younger households, in part because the elderly spend more time at home, and, in part, because familiarity and continuity are more highly valued by older people. As we shall see, this is reflected in significantly lower rates of moving for the elderly.

Federal housing policy, of course, can only go so far in addressing these issues. One dimension of federal policy continuing under the Reagan administration is that housing assistance will not be provided on an entitlement basis; that is, not every household that meets the income and housing eligibility rules will be entitled to assistance. Adding units each year has moved the nation closer to entitlement in housing assistance, but now the government is prepared to halt movement toward this goal. Instead, the administration has proposed limiting federal housing assistance to a fixed number of slots, 3.8 million at the end of fiscal year 1983, for which households must compete.

This raises two basic questions regarding elderly assistance:

- How sensitive to the type of assistance provided is the fraction of the assisted households who are elderly?
- Will changes in the form of assistance provided alter the profile of the types of elderly households that are served?

A large percentage of the elderly households who are currently assisted live in units whose development was subsidized, either being built by the government in the form of public housing or involving one or another of the new construction subsidies to private developers that were offered by the federal government over the years. The share of households in "existing" housing programs who are elderly is much smaller, raising the important question of the ability of the elderly to participate in a system of housing assistance with almost exclusive reliance on the existing stock. How well do the elderly handle their own housing-related problems in the private market? Under housing vouchers, if a unit needs to be repaired for it to qualify under the program's health and safety requirements, the elderly may have to negotiate with their landlords to have their units improved. In other cases, would-be participants have to find a new unit in order to qualify for payments, and, given lower rates of mobility among the elderly than among the nonelderly, there is doubt that this approach will be of much benefit to the elderly. Indeed, it may undermine the system of housing assistance for the elderly.

Beyond these general concerns, the administration's specific voucher proposal requires special analysis. The proposed payment level, the required fraction of income which the household must contribute, how income is counted, and the other specific features of the proposal, all are potentially important design issues that can affect the extent to which the elderly will be served. This report therefore addresses each of the specific program features.

While a central part of this report is an analysis of the impact of the voucher approach on housing assistance, other aspects of the Reagan administration's policies merit examination. For example, several key changes were made in the present programs during the 1981 legislative year. These changes "targeted" assistance more narrowly on those thought to be in greater need by lowering the income limits which define household eligibility in both Section 8 and public housing. Furthermore, tenant contributions to rent, which are determined as a fraction of the household's income, were raised. Both changes, *a priori*, would make participation more difficult; the issue addressed here is whether the elderly were more adversely affected by them. During the same legislative year, changes were made in how income is counted, by moving further in the direction of standardized deductions. One portion of the analysis simulates the impact this change is having on elderly eligibility and participation. These changes are not proposals; they are already in the process of being implemented by the Department of Housing and Urban Development.

Another segment of the analysis considers the likely impact of a proposal which has been included as a part of the administration's voucher package but could well be severed from that package and enacted as a part of the current housing assistance system. This proposal involves counting the value of food stamps as a part of income for determination of eligibility and subsidy level. While there are good arguments why food stamps should be considered like other forms of income on equity grounds, the issue addressed here is the extent to which this rule would further eliminate elderly households from eligibility. Once the overall effect is known, we provide details on the types of elderly households that would suffer from the imposition of this rule.

Two other Reagan administration proposals are not considered here in detail because they appear to involve a small number of units, because their future is uncertain, and because they do not appear to represent the central thrust of federal housing policy. One is the continued funding of the Section 202 program, begun in 1964. This program provides direct loans from the federal government to nonprofit sponsors for the construction of new housing for the elderly and for the nonelderly handicapped. The sponsors build the housing projects, and also manage them once built. Thus, the program is clearly a supply-side program; beginning with units for which funds were appropriated in 1977, however, eligible households also receive assistance in paying their rents through the Section 8 program in addition to the lower rent from the government's interest rate. Unfortunately, very little is known about those who now occupy Section 202 housing, and no reliable data source was available for analysis in this report.

A second proposal is the "Rental Rehabilitation Grant." Again, unlike vouchers, this is a supply-side program meant to augment the availability of rental units. However, many of the details of the administration's proposal were unclear at the time of this work, preventing analysis of its impact. Apparently, communities would be awarded grant money with a great deal of flexibility as to their use. Subsidies to individual units would be limited to some percentage (50 percent is often mentioned) of the rehabilitation costs. There is a link between this program and the voucher program, however, because, at least initially, landlords in the rehabilitated buildings would have to rent some of their units to voucher recipients.

It may strike some that what has not been included in this report is an assessment of the future of assistance to elderly homeowners. Indeed, over the past few years, much more has been learned about elderly homeowners and considerable public attention has been given to this group. However, no new initiatives at the federal level appear to be forthcoming. Under the current Community Development Block Grant program (whose own future seems reasonably secure, albeit at a lower level of funding compared to pre-Reagan budgets) many elderly households have received help in repairing and rehabilitating their homes through loans or grants. Such programs are designed and administered at the local level, and this will very likely continue to be the case. Despite their larger numbers, elderly homeowners have not received the type of programmatic attention at the federal level that renters have. Aside from providing basic background information on the housing circumstances and income of elderly homeowners—as a means of keeping the major topic of this report in perspective—we will not provide new analysis of homeownership programs that are only at the "potential" stage.

In brief, this report provides a careful analsysis of the implications for elderly renters of several major changes in U.S. policy. Because five of every six elderly renters live in an urban area, we have restricted most of our analysis to those living in the nation's standard metropolitan statistical areas.

Overview of the Findings

We now present a brief summary of the findings documented in this report. Information on housing conditions and program participation is summarized by way of background followed by the results of the analysis of the 1981 legislation and the administration's voucher proposal. For the analysis of enacted legislation, we concentrate on eligibility and participation impacts. For the voucher proposal, participation and benefit levels are analyzed.

Housing Conditions of the Elderly. The number of elderly persons in the nation will increase by 50 percent in the last quarter of the twentieth century, and those 75 years of age or over will increase even faster. The majority of the elderly will doubtless continue to live in owner-occupied housing, although tenure status is difficult to predict because of the countervailing effects of changes in the taxing of capital gains on equity in owner-occupied housing and newly available reverse annuity mortgages. It seems fairly safe to predict, however, that elderly renters are likely to remain systematically poorer than owners.

In general, the elderly live in more modest and smaller units than the nonelderly. There are particularly high rates of dwelling deficiencies for units occupied by three elderly groups—blacks, those living in rural areas, and impoverished households. Elderly renters, in general, are more than twice as likely to live in units with two or more defects than are elderly owners. Deficiency rates are persistently high in rural areas, but most elderly renter households (83 percent) live in urban areas, and the majority, mostly women, live alone. It is expected that this pattern will continue in the future.

The average elderly household spends about 23 percent of income for housing expenses, compared to 20 percent for nonelderly households. These averages can be misleading, however, since 22 percent of elderly households spend more than 35 percent. Tenure and poverty status make a big difference. For example, 41 percent of renter households below the official poverty level spend over 45 percent of their income on housing.

Although other aspects of the housing of the elderly differ by income and household type, their mobility rates do not vary much, once tenure is held constant. These rates are consistently only one-third those of the nonelderly.

Participation in Housing Assistance Programs. Roughly 3.1 million households were being served by HUD renter programs by the end of 1980, as the Reagan administration took office. Of these, 40 percent (or 1.2 million) were headed by elderly persons. The Section 202 housing construction program included the highest percentage of elderly—80 percent— although this is understandable since the program is restricted to the elderly and handicapped or disabled nonelderly. The program serving the lowest fraction of elderly was the Section 8 Existing program, although even here one participant in three was elderly. Overall, about 72 percent of all the elderly being assisted resided in units built by the government (public housing) or subsidized through new construction or substantial rehabilitation.

All three of the major programs operating in 1980—public housing, Section 8 Existing, and Section 8 New Construction—served similar types of elderly households with respect to the sex of the head, household composition, and household size. In each program, about three-fourths of elderly households were headed by women, and four-fifths were persons living alone. The major differences in participant profiles lie in race, income, and the proportion that are 75 years of age or older. Public housing serves the largest percentage of elderly blacks, and Section 8 New Construction the least. About 30 percent of the elderly in each component of Section 8 are 75 years of age or older, but a full 45 percent of public housing elderly tenants are in this group, probably reflecting the aging in-place of long-term residents. Average incomes are lower for the elderly than for the nonelderly in all three programs, but they are lowest among the elderly in the public housing program.

Lowering Income Eligibility Limits. Using income eligibility limits in place prior to 1981, about one-third of all households eligible for assistance were elderly. If this is considered a measure of need, the elderly, who constitute about 40 percent of participants, were being served in a proportion greater than their need.

In 1981, Congress lowered the income limit for most housing assistance recipients from 80 percent of area median to 50 percent in an attempt to target assistance more on poorer households. The impact of this change was dramatic. It is predicted that in 1983 the eligible renter population in SMSAs will fall from 49 percent to 28 percent under the new rule. However, the elderly are less affected by the rule. The elderly eligible population is reduced by 32 percent compared to a 45 percent reduction for the nonelderly. Because the elderly were a smaller share of all eligibles to begin with, the new pool of eligible households shifts only slightly in favor of the elderly. The elderly eligibles remain roughly one-third of all eligibles. Thus, they would continue to be served in greater proportion to their need, were no other changes made.

The profile of the elderly eligible population undergoes some change under the new income limit in the direction of greater representation by female-headed and single-person households. Given the results reported above, this appears consistent with the goal of targeting toward more needy groups. In addition, the average income for the eligible elderly is reduced by about 25 percent as a result of the new income limit, further justifying the new rule.

Despite regulations to protect current participants from being eliminated, in the long term the 50 percent of income limit will affect the characteristics of participating households. A quarter of 1983 participants would be excluded on the basis of this rule change alone, to be replaced eventually by households below 50 percent of area median income. Estimates show that the directions of change are similar to those observed for the eligible population, with female-headed and single-person elderly households being served more.

Reducing the income eligibility limit, however, accentuates a "notch" problem in the way the subsidy schedule is calculated. Some households with a dollar more of income become ineligible for benefits, because the schedule is no longer smooth (reducing gradually to zero as income increases). This "notch" in the schedule creates strong incentives to underreport income, work less, or sell assets at below market rates, or give them to children in order to qualify for payments. It is not known how many elderly households will react in these ways.

Standardizing Deductions. The 1981 legislation standardized deductions uniformly for the Section 8 and public housing programs for the purpose of adjusting income used to determine subsidy levels. Only 1 percent of all participating households in 1983 would have their eligibility affected by the new deductions ($400 for each minor, and $300 for each elderly-headed household). The new deductions are slightly more generous on average to both groups of households.

Increasing Tenant Rent Contributions. By increasing the rent contribution for participants from 25 to 30 percent of adjusted income, some households will no longer be eligible because their benefits will be reduced to zero. About 11 percent of those who would have been participating in rental assistance programs in 1983 will be eliminated from eligibility in the long run, as this rule takes full effect. There is no difference between the percentage of elderly and nonelderly who lose eligibility through this method of decreasing subsidy levels.

Counting Food Stamps. Although counting food stamps as a part of household income is an element of the administration's entire housing assistance package for the future, its separate impact is analyzed in this report.

The change would affect both eligibility and participation. About 4 percent of the eligible population would become ineligible because their incomes would be too high, although there is no difference in this result between elderly and nonelderly households. Because the value of food stamps rises as the household's income declines, counting food stamps increases the average income of the poorest household more. This results in less targeting to the neediest households rather than more.

The impact of counting food stamps would be comparatively greater on the participating population than on the eligible population. About 6 percent of 1983 participants would have incomes too high to continue to qualify for payments. Elderly households would be affected somewhat less (about 5 percent) and nonelderly households would be affected somewhat more (about 8 percent).

Implementing Housing Vouchers. The elderly would get the largest share of subsidy resources if future housing assistance policy were similar to pre-Reagan years, i.e., characterized by a substantial share of new construction projects set aside for occupancy by the elderly and the elderly competing with other households for the remaining program slots. If policy moved instead toward complete reliance on the Section 8 Existing program, *as it is now structured,* the elderly would be in a difficult competitive position, because nonelderly households would be strongly motivated to participate by benefits large enough for them to get their landlords to fix up their dwellings, or to induce them to move to a new unit in order to qualify.

The voucher proposal by the administration has a sharply lower benefit structure than the current Section 8 Existing program—elderly individual's benefits, for example, fall by 51 percent. This program lies somewhere in between the status quo and exclusive reliance on the current Section 8 Existing program in terms of the share of program benefits that would go to the elderly. The elderly are more likely to live in dwelling units that qualify at enrollment. Moreover, those elderly who live in a unit not meeting the program's physical standard at enrollment are less sensitive to the size of subsidy payment they would receive if they qualified than the nonelderly. Hence, they are more likely to eventually receive assistance than the nonelderly are. Thus, while the benefit to individual elderly households will be much smaller under the proposed program, the share of participating households that will be elderly will be larger.

Experience in testing the voucher concept suggests some additional differences between the elderly and nonelderly that should be kept in mind in designing a voucher program. The elderly are less likely to hear about such a program, holding other factors constant; and they are less likely to enroll once they know about it. This suggests that outreach to the elderly may be important in some areas, even under a nonentitlement program. Furthermore, the likelihood of the elderly actually qualifying for payments (compared to the nonelderly) can be influenced by significant changes in the stringency of the physical standards applied to dwelling units. Assuming that the standards will remain about the same as they are in the current Section 8 program, the results predicted above for the elderly under the administration's voucher program should not be affected: they will constitute a larger share of program participants than under the Section 8 Existing program. The voucher program, thus, will perpetuate the pattern of a disproportionate share of elderly renters being served by federal housing assistance programs.

Structure of this Report

This report is divided into six chapters. The next chapter provides background information on the housing of the elderly population. Attention is given to present trends as well as to future projections. This chapter paints a picture of the overall degree to which the elderly could use assistance, and provides relief to that picture by examining the circumstances of various subgroups within the elderly population.

Chapter three then compiles the best evidence available on how elderly renters were served by federal programs prior to 1981. More detail is provided on renters in urban areas, in part because of data availability, and in part because most elderly renters live in such areas. Important statistics that are presented in this chapter include the percentage who are elderly within each program. Furthermore, the important differences in what types of elderly households are served by different programs are presented.

Chapter four analyzes the impact of the 1981 legislative changes—that are gradually being implemented—on eligibility levels within the population and the impact on the continued eligibility of current program participants. Several data sources are used for these calculations in order to increase the reliability of the estimates. Chapter five follows in much the same vein, with analysis of the effects on eligibility and participation in having assistance programs count food stamps as income, as the administration proposes.

Chapter six represents the most important analyses for future policy making. We reexamine the evidence from the Experimental Housing Allowance Program, which tested several variations of the voucher idea in twelve sites between 1973 and 1980. Using data from these experiments, we report new analyses on the likely impact of vouchers on elderly participation. As importantly, this chapter addresses the voucher question from another perspective: if vouchers are taken as a certainty for the future, then how should they be designed to insure that the elderly are assisted?

Chapter 2

THE ELDERLY AND THEIR HOUSING

Evaluating housing assistance programs for the elderly requires an understanding of the basic housing circumstances that the elderly face. It must be recognized first of all that the housing situation of the elderly differs from that of their younger counterparts. The housing and neighborhood environment is of greater importance to the elderly than to other households because of the greater proportion of time the elderly spend at home and in their immediate neighborhoods. Another distinguishing characteristic of the housing consumption of the elderly is the frequent changes in the determinants of the optimal set or bundle of housing services that they would prefer to consume. From numerous studies of housing demand, we know that the preferred set depends on such factors as income level and asset holdings, household size and composition, and the health status of its members.

Among the elderly, these determinants can be expected to change, sometimes in rapid succession. One's spouse may die, functional mobility may become impaired, or income may be reduced by the inflationary erosion of the value of some assets. How each of these changes affects housing demand depends, of course, on the broader family environment. The onset of activity limitations for the male in a husband-wife household will have little effect, if the spouse is able to effectively compensate for the housekeeping functions performed by her husband and tend to his now greater needs without undue strain. The onset of the limitations to someone living alone, however, requires the installation of special features—grab bars, specialized sink hardware, and so forth—to make continued independent living feasible.

The determinants of the preferred bundle of housing services interact powerfully with a third characteristic of the elderly: their lower propensity to make major housing adjustments. The low average mobility rates of elderly Americans is well known. These reflect the strong social ties and sense of place attachment built up over the course of decades which the elderly are understandably loath to disturb. Hence, adjustments are often gradual. Homeowners in large dwellings who cannot afford to consume so much housing, may reduce maintenance or postpone making needed replacements. Renters in similar circumstances may continue to live in a unit, but only at the cost of spending inordinate shares of their incomes to do so.

A final characteristic of the elderly's housing is that the definition of "housing" is broader than that typically used. For the elderly one must ask if the dwelling and its associated neighborhood are usable by the occupant. Beyond knowing that the unit is equipped with a serviceable bathtub and hot and cold water, one must know whether or not the members of the household can use it—completely independently, with special equipment, or with personal assistance. An upstairs bedroom is of little use if its intended nocturnal occupant is incapable of negotiating the stairs. There is little systematic information on special dwelling adaptations and intrahousehold services provided to compensate for health and activity limitations. Nevertheless, a "livability" standard is key to thinking about the housing of the elderly.

This chapter provides some essential background information for interpreting the material presented later on the responses of the elderly to the offer of housing assistance; that is, the extent of their participation in assistance programs. Like the rest of the volume, the emphasis is on the elderly who live in rental accommodations, although data are also provided on homeowners for reference.

Three topics are taken up in turn below. First, the salient factors determining housing consumption are quantified, and differences among the elderly in various situations documented. Both the current situation and changes expected in the future are described for household composition, living arrangements, and household income. The housing situation of the elderly, as defined by housing quality and housing expense burden, is then briefly described. Finally, the mobility experience of the elderly in recent years is outlined.

Population, Living Arrangements, and Income: Present and Future

The increasing importance of older persons in the nation's population is a widely appreciated fact. The number of persons 65 years of age and older will increase from 22 to 33 million between 1975 and 2010, a 50 percent jump (see table 2-1). The population 75 years of age and over will increase even more over the same period, that is, by 64 percent, and will then constitute 5 percent of the total population. The approximately 14 million persons 75

TABLE 2-1
THE NUMBER OF PERSONS IN THE OLDER AGES, 1975–2010

	Number of Persons[a]			*Percent of Total Population in Age Group*		
Age Group	*1975*	*1990*	*2010*	*1975*	*1990*	*2010*
55 years and over	42.2	49.4	65.7	19.7	20.0	23.6
65 years and over	22.4	28.9	33.2	10.5	11.7	11.9
75 years and over	8.5	11.4	13.9	4.0	4.7	5.0

SOURCE: U.S. Bureau of the Census (1976), tables 2-1, 2-4.

a. In millions.

years of age or older expected to be present in 2010 are especially important when considering the effects of new policy directions on the elderly, because this group is especially vulnerable to health problems that can affect the type of housing that is appropriate.

Actually, the increase in the number of cohorts of "young-old" (persons aged 65 to 74) and of "old-old" (75 and over) will follow an uneven trajectory in the decades ahead. The number of young-old is rising rapidly—by 20 percent per decade—during the 1970–1990 period (and will do so again beginning in 2030). The number of old-old by contrast will increase by about 20 percent per decade each decade from 1970 to 2000. Thus, the old-old will become an increasing share of the elderly population for the next 30 years, reaching 42 percent of all persons over age 65 in 2010 (i.e., (13.9/33.2) * 100). This pattern is important because the old-old group is considered to be more vulnerable in terms of health status. Clearly, this is not a perfect substitute for information on health-related factors that can directly affect how the elderly are housed, but it does differentiate the elderly in terms of their probability of health-related problems, and does so in a consistent way across data bases, (For more on this, see Newman, Zais, Struyk, forthcoming.)

The passage of time will also witness changes in the marital status of the elderly, as illustrated by the figures in table 2-2. In particular, higher divorce rates among the nonelderly in past years and higher life expectancy among males causes some notable alterations to the 1975 distribution of the elderly by marital status. By 1990, more elderly men will still be living with their wives: 77 vs. 75 percent for those age 65 to 74, and 65 vs. 60 percent for those over age 75. Obviously, a similar pattern holds for women. However, even though at every age more of the elderly will be in marriages, higher mortality rates of males as age rises means that there will be little change in

TABLE 2-2
DISTRIBUTION OF THE POPULATION 55 YEARS OLD AND OVER BY MARITAL STATUS, 1975 AND 1990

	Male			*Female*		
Year and Marital Status	*55 to 64 years*	*65 to 74 years*	*75 years and over*	*55 to 64 years*	*65 to 74 years*	*75 years and over*
1975						
Single	8	8	7	7	8	8
Married	85	78	64	67	45	21
spouse present	82	75	60	64	44	19
spouse absent	3	3	4	4	2	2
Widowed	4	11	27	21	44	70
Divorced	3	3	1	4	3	1
1990						
Single	4	7	4	5	7	6
Married with spouse present	85	77	65	70	46	20
Other ever married	10	16	30	25	47	74

SOURCE: U.S. Bureau of the Census (1976), table 6-1.

the share of elderly women living outside of marriage. In 1990, 34 percent of men and 80 percent of women over age 75 will be living without a spouse, because they never married or because their marriage has ended for any reason; the parallel figures for 1975 were 40 percent of men and 81 percent of women.

The relationship between marital status and tenure is worth exploring. In 1978, 15 million households were maintained by persons 65 years old and over. In table 2-3, we show the tenure and living arrangements for these and younger households by age cohort. The top panel of the table shows that the elderly households as a group are overwhelmingly owner-occupants; about three-fourths own the houses they live in. This panel also shows that the rate of homeownership declines steadily as age increases, from an 80 percent rate for those age 55 to 64 to a 69 percent rate for those 75 years old and over.

The bottom panel allows us to examine the tenure split for each household type. Interestingly, the rate of homeownership declines for elderly headed families as age increases, but it increases for males living alone and remains about constant for females living alone. The patterns for those living alone are presumably due to an increasing number of surviving spouses continuing to live in the home they previously occupied with their spouses. However,

TABLE 2-3
DISTRIBUTION OF ELDERLY HOUSEHOLDS BY TENURE AND OF HOUSEHOLD TYPE BY AGE OF HEAD, 1978

	Age of Head		
	55 to 64	*65 to 74*	*75 and over*
Tenure			
Homeowners	80	73	69
Renters	20	27	31
Household Type by Tenure			
Homeowners			
Families	83	67	52
Living alone			
male	4	6	11
female	12	27	37
Renters			
Families	52	37	30
Living alone			
male	17	16	14
female	30	47	56
Tenure by Household Type			
Families			
Owners	86	85	80
Renters	14	15	20
Males living alone			
Owners	22	32	45
Renters	78	68	55
Females living alone			
Owners	59	62	60
Renters	41	38	40

SOURCE: U.S. Bureau of the Census (1979), table 33.

there is a large enough number of widows who shift to rental status as they age for the total growth in the number of renters to increase relative to the number of owner-occupants; this accounts for the rise in share of all elderly households who are renters as one looks at successive cohorts.

Library
St. Joseph's College
Patchogue, N.Y. 11772

The center panel of the table addresses the household composition of homeowners and renters. Two points stand out immediately. First, the majority of renters over age 65 live alone; and among those living alone, women outnumber men about three to one. Second, the proportion of the renters living alone is higher for the old-old than for the young-old: 70 percent vs. 63 percent. The majority of homeowners, on the other hand, are families, even for the old-old.

What type of dwelling units do these households occupy today, and what will the likely situation be in the year 2000? To answer this question we rely on the set of demographic projections to the year 2000 recently completed by Pitkin and Masnick (1979). The truly distinguishing aspect of these projections is that they have been related to past housing preferences (i.e., actual housing choices), in order to construct probable distributions of tenure and structure types of households of various ages in the year 2000.

The Pitkin-Masnick projections were done by age, sex, marital status, and (for women) children ever born. Three distinct sets of projections were made, based on particular assumptions about the future trajectories of marital status and fertility. The basic methodology was to age the different cohorts forward in time and redistribute the survivors among marital status and headship (male vs. female) categories. (Women are distributed among categories of children ever born as well.) The beginning date for the projections is 1976, and the projections were made at five-year intervals for the 1980-2000 period. The results reported in the following paragraphs are based on the median fertility assumption used: total fertility rate of 1.8 after 1980.

Two alternative housing projection series were used by Pitkin and Masnick to bracket the range of likely trajectories of actual housing consumption patterns. The first is based on the assumption that household preferences for various housing bundles will remain fixed, as observed in 1975. These bundle choices are defined by tenure, structure type, and number of room combinations for 20 specific household types, defined by sex, marital status, and number of children.

The second series is based on more complex assumptions, reflecting the trends in housing consumption patterns actually observed for birth cohorts during the 1960–1975 period. For each 5-year birth cohort in the projections, the rates of change in housing consumption patterns over each 5-year interval are equal to the average of the rates of change for cohorts who passed through the same age interval between 1960 and 1975. As an example, the rate of homeownership among those who will be age 70–74 in 1980 depends on (1) the rate of homeownership among those who were 65–69 years old in 1975, and (2) the average rate at which earlier cohorts increased their homeownership rate between ages 65–69 and 70–74. All of these rates were projected separately for each of the household types within each cohort. Note that the extrapolation projections include the rate at which the elderly have been "uncoupling" from living with children or other arrangements; for this reason, the total count of elderly headed households increases under this assumption.

The analysis presented here uses only a very small part of the full projections done by Pitkin and Masnick. Table 2-4 displays the 1976 distribution of households headed by a person 65 or older by tenure status and the number of dwelling units in the structure occupied by such households. As expected, the majority of homeowners lived in single unit structures in 1976; less expected, perhaps, is that the most common form of accommodations rented by the elderly are in large (five or more units) structures. Under the constant housing preference assumption, there is little change in those patterns over the period. However, under the "extrapolated preferences" the share of homeowners increases from 68 to 73 percent and the importance of renting

TABLE 2-4
DISTRIBUTION OF HOUSEHOLDS HEADED BY PERSON 65 OR OLDER BY TENURE AND STRUCTURE TYPE, 1976 AND 2000, UNDER ALTERNATIVE ASSUMPTIONS ABOUT HOUSING PREFERENCES

	1976	*2000 (constant preference assumptions)*	*2000 (extrapolation preference assumptions)*
Owner-occupants	68	67	73
Single unit	58	57	59
2–4 units	5	5	4
5 + units	2	2	2
Mobile home	3	3	8
Renters	32	33	27
Single unit	9	9	7
2–4 units	8	9	7
5 + units	14	15	12
Mobile home	6	a	1
Total	100	100	100

SOURCE: Pitkin and Masnick (1979).

a. Less than one-half of 1 percent.

declines accordingly. The only other changes of note are the increased importance of mobile homes for owner-occupants and the decline of renters.

It is important to realize that this projected increase in homeownership assumes that other factors, not accounted for in the assumptions, remain roughly the same over the period. One major change, for example, has been the exemption of capital gains on home equity from federal taxation for persons 55 years of age and older through the 1978 tax legislation. This surely will encourage some shifting to rental status beyond that which would normally occur. On the other hand, the potential widespread availability of reverse annuity mortgages, which would help the "housing poor" to remain in their homes, could offset this factor. Moreover, those predictions assume a steady increase in the incomes of the elderly to offset inflation.

Certainly, the income status of the elderly is a key determinant of housing consumption, no matter what the future of factors like those cited above. Whenever discussing the incomes of the elderly, two strong cautions are in order. One is that households make many of their major decisions, including whether or not to purchase their own home, on the basis of their long term or permanent income. Income typically falls significantly at retirement to a level below the permanent one which was applicable when such decisions were made. One indication of the importance of permanent income comes from the share of elderly who are homeowners at lower income levels (see table 2-5). Even a majority of elderly with annual incomes below $3,000 owned their houses in 1977. At $7,000 income per year about three-quarters are homeowners. Furthermore, as the table suggests, large percentages of all lower income homeowners (at various income levels) are elderly. The second point is that incomes reported in surveys typically exclude the value of government-provided goods and services—assisted housing, medical assistance, and food stamps are prime examples. Hence, the extent of the disparity in the standard of living between higher and lower income figures is overstated by income data. In short, figures on current incomes offer a quite imperfect guide to the full revenue situation of the elderly.

Nonetheless, there are large differences in the current incomes of the elderly, as indicated by the figures in table 2-6 on the median incomes by household type and tenure. For every household type, homeowners have higher incomes than renters. Also, families always have higher incomes than persons living alone, and the difference is large enough to more than compensate for the larger household size.[1] Thus, the lowest income elderly households, as a group, are those living alone in rental housing. Such households have incomes that are about one half of those of elderly headed homeowner families. Table 2-6 also provides separate figures for elderly black households. In all cases the median incomes of blacks is less than that of the "average"

TABLE 2-5
TENURE BY INCOME AND AGE OF HOUSEHOLD HEAD IN 1977

	Homeownership Rates			*Elderly Headed Households as a Percentage of*	
Annual Income	*All Households*	*Elderly Headed Households*	*Other Households*	*Homeowners*	*Renters*
Under $3,000	43	53	33	48	32
3,000–4,999	47	61	32	65	36
5,000–6,999	51	73	37	54	21
7,000–9,999	53	78	44	39	12
10,000–12,499	58	83	54	21	6
12,500–14,999	66	84	64	16	6
15,000–19,999	72	85	71	10	4
20,000–24,999	81	86	80	6	4
25,000–34,000	86	86	87	5	6
35,000 +	90	88	90	7	8

SOURCE: Struyk (1981a), table 2.

TABLE 2-6
MEDIAN INCOMES OF ELDERLY HEADED HOUSEHOLDS
BY TENURE AND HOUSEHOLD TYPE, 1979

	All Races		*Blacks*	
Household Type	*Owner-Occupants*	*Renters*	*Owner-Occupants*	*Renters*
2-or-more Person Households				
Husband-wife Families	$11,100	$8,800	$7,600	$6,000
Other Male-headed Families	11,600	6,900	7,600	a
Other Female-headed Families	10,300	7,000	7,000	5,500
1-person Households				
Male	6,300	5,100	5,400	4,200
Female	5,400	4,700	3,200	3,000

SOURCE: U.S. Bureau of the Census, Annual Housing Survey (1981), table A-1.

a. Data not available.

household in each tenure and household type cell. The median income of black women living alone as renters is especially low. These women account for 17 percent of all elderly black households.

A more general picture of the incidence of poverty among the elderly defined by tenure and living arrangements is given in table 2-7. Looking first at the data for all races combined, the distinction by tenure is less crucial than living arrangement, although poverty rates are higher for renters; those living alone or with nonrelatives have a much higher likelihood of being impoverished. Among blacks the incidence of poverty is typically twice that of all households; in fact, more than half of elderly blacks living alone have current incomes below the poverty line.

The trajectory of future incomes of the elderly is a basic parameter in thinking about housing policy. To the extent that incomes are expected to decline, the quality of housing can be expected to decline or certainly not improve. Wertheimer and Zedlewski (1978) have made projections of the change to 1990 from 1976 in the incomes of the elderly under two alternative scenarios about the extent of involvement in the labor force by elderly households.

In one projection—termed the "Low Participation Scenario"—it was assumed that the combination of a slowly growing economy and continuation of the current Social Security benefit structure would perpetuate past trends, which have led to less and less labor force participation by the elderly. Thus, in this scenario the labor force participation rate, hours worked, and earnings of the elderly continue to fall as they did during the last 20 years.

In the other projection—termed the "High Participation Scenario"—it was assumed that the past trends which have led to less and less labor force participation by the elderly would be reversed through a combination of changes in government macroeconomic policy, changes in the Social Security benefit structure, an increase in the mandatory retirement age, and the changing demographic structure of the population.

In light of the inflation and employment rates over the 1979–1981 period, the assumptions underlying these projections seem very optimistic indeed.[2] Although they provide a rough indication of the range of change in the next decade, any increases projected probably should be adjusted downward to account for the higher rates of inflation experienced. Table 2-8 summarizes the actual projections. The right-hand panel combines changes in Social Security benefits and earnings to give a composite picture. Under both scenarios, all three household types—married families and male and female individuals—enjoy some increase in real incomes. For individuals in the 65–69 age group under the Low Participation Scenario, the gains are very small and likely to evaporate completely under the present economic conditions. Elderly

TABLE 2-7

NUMBER AND PERCENTAGE OF ELDERLY BELOW THE POVERTY LEVEL, BY RACE AND SELECTED CHARACTERISTICS[a]

Characteristics	All Races		White		Black	
	Total	Percent Below Poverty	Total	Percent Below Poverty	Total	Percent Below Poverty
Owner-Occupied Units	10,647	14.7	9,845	13.1	725	35.0
Family	6,690	7.6	6,152	6.1	482	24.9
Unrelated Individuals						
Males	781	19.0	716	16.9	59	b
Females	3,176	28.7	2,977	26.7	184	59.2
Living Alone	3,813	26.9	3,571	25.0	223	56.1
Renter Occupied Units	4,170	26.8	3,608	23.9	514	46.9
Family	1,439	15.0	1,201	11.5	211	24.9
Unrelated Individuals						
Males	614	31.2	497	28.1	109	47.9
Females	2,117	33.4	1,910	30.6	194	61.2
Living Alone	2,670	33.0	2,357	30.3	292	55.8

SOURCE: U.S. Bureau of the Census, "Characteristics of the Population Below the Poverty Level: 1976," Current Population Reports. Series P-60, No. 115, July 1978, tables 8, 9, 11, and 24. Elderly defined as 65+ years of age.

a. Number in thousands

b. Base less than 75,000.

TABLE 2-8
CHANGE IN REAL BENEFITS AND NET EARNINGS: 1977 to 1990
(1976 DOLLARS)

	Social Security Benefits			*Net Earnings*			*Total (Benefits + Earnings)*		
		Change: 1977 to 1990			*Change: 1977 to 1990*			*Change: 1977 to 1980*	
	Mean 1977 Level	*Low Partici-pation*	*High Partici-pation*	*Mean 1977 Level*	*Low Partici-pation*	*High Partici-pation*	*Mean 1977 Level*	*Low Partici-pation*	*High Partici-pation*
Married Families									
Age: 62–64	$2,449	+77%	+49%	$8,277	+ 5%	+56%	$10,726	+21%	+55%
65–69	4,372	+37	+32	3,458	−17	+49	7,830	+13	+39
70+	4,618	+21	+22	1,524	− 5	+48	6,142	+15	+28
Single: Male-Headed Families									
Age: 62–64	$1,912	+55%	+42%	$3,395	+26%	+123%	$5,307	+36%	+81%
65–69	2,888	+34	+28	1,833	−47	+ 64	4,721	+ 3	+42
70+	2,516	+26	+29	1,063	−23	+ 28	3,579	+12	+29
Single: Female-Headed Families									
Age: 62–64	$1,452	+23%	+23%	$3,210	+16%	+24%	$4,662	+18%	+24%
65–69	2,262	+12	+ 7	1,055	−16	+ 5	3,317	+ 3	+ 6
70+	2,270	+23	+23	156	−21	+67	2,426	+21	+25

SOURCE: Wertheimer and Zedlewski (1978).

headed families, on the other hand, are likely to prosper under this scenario. With greater attachment to the labor force, spurred by a change to Social Security that makes early retirement less attractive and raises the benefits of late retirement, incomes are generally higher. This outcome is to be expected, given the relatively higher incomes of the employed compared to those relying exclusively on retirement income.

With the Reagan administration's current (1982) policy of leaving Social Security alone, the second scenario is less likely. Thus, on balance, little real income growth for the elderly until 1990 is in prospect. This, if coupled with reduction in in-kind assistance such as housing, would mean a clear reduction in the economic resources enjoyed by the elderly.

The Current Housing Situation

Three aspects of the housing situation of the aged are documented in this section: (1) the physical characteristics of the dwellings occupied, with special emphasis on a set of conditions commonly accepted as being deficiencies; (2) the housing expense burden, defined as the percentage of current income spent on housing services, and (3) the location of the elderly in urban and rural areas. This section explores these aspects in considerable detail providing facts which are essential for the discussion of housing assistance in the remainder of this study.

The data employed are mainly from the 1976 and 1979 Annual Housing Survey, a national survey of approximately 70,000 dwelling units that has been fielded by the Department of Housing and Urban Development and the Bureau of the Census since 1973. Each year an enumerator returns to the same group of dwelling units, thus creating a longitudinal record for those households which have not relocated. The survey as a whole gives a longitudinal record of the entire housing stock, including demolitions and new construction.

Not all of the elderly are included in our tabulations. The study excludes those elderly who are living in a dependent status and are not designated as heads of households, such as the widow living in her daughter's household; in this case the quality of her housing depends heavily on the housing preferences of her daughter and son-in-law. Our data also exclude persons living in group quarters, such as boarding houses, as well as those living in institutions. The present focus is on the relation between the economic and personal resources of the elderly and their physical environment. We have termed the subpopulation studied here the "independent elderly" in an attempt to keep the distinction before the reader.

The population of independent elderly is disaggregated along several different lines in the data tabulations presented below: homeowners and renters are distinguished; households are separated into three types (husband-wife families, individuals living alone, and individuals living with nonspouse relatives and/or nonrelatives); and units occupied by blacks and whites are contrasted.

In some instances, households are divided into a three-class system based on current incomes: those in poverty, those between the poverty cutoff and 200 percent of the poverty cutoff, and those with incomes greater than twice the poverty definition. Poverty is defined for each household size in urban and rural areas.

Finally, two geographic classifications are employed, including the four census regions and a metropolitan vs. nonmetropolitan distinction. With these various disaggregations a picture of the current situation and recent trends in the housing of the elderly emerges.

Dwelling Quality

Traditionally, discussions of housing conditions focused on the small set of deficiency measures collected in the decennial census because these data were available and because the indicators corresponded to widely held views about what constituted acceptable housing. Thus three factors were (and still are) regarded as "the bottom line:" (1) incomplete plumbing, that is, not having available one or more of hot and cold piped water, a tub or shower, and a toilet for the exclusive use of the household; (2) overcrowding, generally defined as more than one person per room; and (3) dilapidated condition of the structure. A dilapidated unit is defined by the Census Bureau as one that does not provide safe and adequate shelter and, in its present condition, endangers the health, safety, or well-being of the occupants. Examples of defects that result in such a classification include holes, open cracks, or rotted, loose, or missing materials over large areas of the foundation, outside walls, roof, or inside walls, and so on, or substantial sagging of structural members. Shacks, huts, tents, and similar units can also be classified as dilapidated.

There was a high incidence of all three of these factors in the housing stock in 1950 when such data were first collected. With a decrease in their incidence, many housing professionals have come to take a broader view of the services provided by housing. On the structural side, in addition to the minimum health and safety requirements embodied in the old census definition, the flow of services yielded by the structure and component systems has become critical. Thus, in addition to having complete plumbing, it is equally important that it work dependably. Similarly, it is not only the number and size of the rooms in the dwelling that matter, but also the condition of the walls, ceilings, and floors. The more dependable the systems, the greater the structural integrity, and the better the physical condition, the greater the flow of services provided by the unit.

Each dwelling also has a set of neighborhood attributes associated with it including the condition of the neighbors' dwellings, the conditions of the block front, and the public services provided in the area. If there is any doubt as to whether or not households value such neighborhood attributes, one need merely compare the sales prices of similar dwelling units in different school districts.

Here, we follow a strategy of concentrating on determining the number of elderly persons who live in dwellings that fall below some standard of minimally acceptable housing. An attempt to calculate this number immediately raises the problem of defining "minimally acceptable housing," a formidable issue since there is no widespread agreement even on what should be included in such a standard, or which set within the many that can be constructed using the Annual Housing Survey data is appropriate.

Three approaches to choosing a set of indicators are available. The first is to examine the results of various regression analyses that "explain" the variation in gross rents or house values in terms of the physical attributes of the unit (among other factors) and use those attributes which have a statistically significant negative effect on rents or values. While this approach holds forth something of an ideal, the techniques used to develop data seem too crude to capture a number of important factors.

The second approach is to rely on preferences of society at large. One begins with a cohort of households for whom it is reasonable to assume that current income is close to "long run" or normal income. When the housing of cohorts of households with successively higher incomes are contrasted, one observes a reduction in those "housing deficiencies" that society finds most objectionable. This particular method has been used previously in studying the housing of the elderly and is fairly successful. A problem with previous applications is that, in addition to deficiencies being eliminated as income rises, "luxury" items entered—for example, air conditioning. The result is a list too inclusive for a number of purposes.

The third approach, and the one followed in this study, is to include deficiencies that would disqualify the dwelling for assistance under the Section 8 program, as administered by the Department of Housing and Urban Development. The items included in the Section 8 standard certainly do not include luxury items. Use of these as quality indicators also has the benefit of pointing out what fraction of units could be brought into the nation's largest assisted housing program after some repair or rehabilitation work had been completed.

Table 2-9 defines six indicators used in this study. Note that some have several parts. Although these indicators do not exhaust the list of standards a unit would have to pass to participate in the program, they do include those that appear to best measure a low level of housing services or chronic disruptions in services and that would require nontrivial investments to correct.

One way to judge the reasonableness of using these criteria is to look at how the flow of services provided by a dwelling is affected by the presence of one or more of the deficiencies. A crude measure for rental units is the level of gross rents. Such figures suggest that households place a lower value on rental units where services are made unavailable because of the deficiencies as defined in table 2-9.

Table 2-10 presents data on the quality of housing occupied by the elderly in 1976. Most of the figures are for renters, the focus of our study. The mass of figures may appear impenetrable, but when the data for specific groups are examined separately, a set of conclusions emerges.

Elderly vs. Nonelderly. Panel A of table 2-10 clearly shows that the elderly have a higher incidence of incomplete plumbing and kitchen facilities,

TABLE 2-9
INDICATORS OF HOUSING INADEQUACY

Variable Name	*Description*
Plumbing	Unit either lacks complete plumbing facilities or household must share their use.
Kitchen	Unit either lacks a complete kitchen or household must share their use.
Sewage	One or more of the following three services was unavailable or completely unusable for six or more hours at least three times during the past 90 days: (1) running water, (2) sewage system, (3) toilet.
Heat	The heating system was completely unusable for six or more hours at least three times during the past winter.
Maintenance	Two or more of the following four conditions exist: (1) leaking roof, (2) substantial cracks or holes in walls and ceilings, (3) holes in floors, (4) broken plaster or peeling paint in areas larger than one square foot.
Public Halls	The unit is in a building with public hallways and stairs, and at least two of the following three conditions exist: (1) missing light fixtures, (2) stair railings are missing or poorly attached, (3) missing, loose, or broken steps.

a basic structural deficiency. Six percent of elderly renters have incomplete plumbing and 5 percent lack complete kitchens. Elderly and nonelderly are about evenly matched for heating system and sewage breakdowns; for maintenance deficiencies the results are clearly mixed, with elderly renters having fewer deficiencies than their nonelderly counterparts.

Elderly Owners vs. Elderly Renters. Renters' units have these deficiencies at about twice the rate as do those of homeowners. Lack of complete kitchens, heating breakdowns, and poor maintenance are especially difficult problems for renters compared to homeowners.

Household Type. Among the three household types distinguished—husband-wife, single persons, and other—those in the ''other'' category have the greatest incidence of deficiencies. Husband-wife households exhibit the lowest incidence, with single-person households the second lowest. The stronger economic position of ''other'' households noted earlier makes this result somewhat surprising, but it could be explained by the joint income of the household—which may be two ''partners'' living together—and may not actually indicate the income available to the householder for meeting housing expenses.

Location. Two location breakouts are presented: the four census regions (panel B-4), and units located within and outside of metropolitan areas (panel B-5). The variation among regions is striking for the three deficiencies for which there are generally reliable data—plumbing, kitchen, and maintenance. The South has the greatest incidence of these deficiencies; the West has the least. For kitchens and plumbing, the incidence in the South is nearly twice that of the next worst region, with deficiency rates of 8 and 12 percent, respectively; for maintenance, the South and the Northeast have similar high rates compared to the North Central and West.

The incidence of deficiencies for plumbing and kitchens for elderly households living outside of metropolitan areas is several times the incidence of those living within metropolitan areas. Fourteen percent of nonmetropolitan elderly renters do not have complete plumbing facilities in their units; in metropolitan areas it is 4 percent. The differences for the other deficiencies are much more modest, but the problems of the nonmetropolitan South are pervasively evident.

Race. Elderly blacks exhibit a very high incidence of housing deficiencies (panel B-2). Fourteen percent of black single-person renters live in units not having complete plumbing facilities and 11 percent do not have fully equipped kitchens. The most poorly housed black group is ''other'' renters: one in five lives in a unit with plumbing deficiencies and one in seven lives in a unit

TABLE 2-10
RATES OF SELECTED DWELLING DEFICIENCIES FOR ELDERLY HOUSEHOLDS: 1976[a]
(Percentages)

Panels A and B	*Plumbing*	*Kitchen*	*Sewage*	*Heat*	*Maintenance*	*Public Hallways*
A. Elderly vs. Nonelderly						
Owners						
Elderly	3.28	1.63	.29	.35	2.04	c
Nonelderly	1.08	.60	.32	.38	1.94	c
Renters						
Elderly	6.38	5.22	.57	2.01	6.26	1.29
Nonelderly	3.28	2.72	.87	1.91	8.27	.75
B. Elderly Renters						
1. Household Type						
Husband-wife	4.17	2.03	b	2.60	6.25	b
Single person	7.03	6.48	.57	1.87	5.86	.70
Other	7.76	5.26	.52	b	8.67	b
2. Race						
Husband-wife						
black	13.91	b	b	b	19.64	b
nonblack	2.92	1.54	b	2.24	4.53	b
Singles						
black	13.64	11.18	b	3.93	13.62	b
nonblack	6.18	5.58	b	1.61	4.87	.64
Other						
black	20.49	14.61	b	b	15.50	b
nonblack	4.63	b	b	b	6.85	b

3. Poverty						
Husband-wife						
below poverty	13.43	6.42	b	b	11.46	b
pov to twice pov	4.14	b	b	b	6.74	b
over twice pov	b	b	b	2.64	4.02	b
Singles						
below poverty	11.86	7.60	b	1.91	7.53	b
pov to twice pov	4.59	5.42	b	1.91	5.27	b
over twice pov	4.49	6.92	b	b	4.44	b
Other						
below poverty	13.46	8.24	b	b	10.28	b
pov to twice pov	8.54	6.36	b	b	10.16	b
over twice pov	b	b	b	b	b	b
4. Location Region						
Northwest	4.22	4.60	1.20	4.34	7.36	1.02
North Central	5.94	3.60	b	b	4.27	b
South	11.84	8.54	b	1.58	9.00	1.01
West	2.81	3.55	b	b	2.87	b
5. Metro Status						
in metro area	3.92	4.29	b	2.28	5.80	.84
outside metro area	14.51	8.21	b	1.10	7.65	b

SOURCE: Struyk and Soldo (1980), Table 3-6.

a. Definitions appear in table 2.9.
b. Number in sample too small to be statistically reliable.
c. Not computed for owners.

with incomplete kitchen facilities or maintenance deficiencies. In 1976, there were only about 88,000 households in this category, and it would indeed be a challenge to find the 20,000 most in need. On the other hand, the problems among elderly blacks are so pervasive that simply assisting them as a group would sacrifice little in terms of program efficiency.

Poverty Status. Panel B-3 exhibits the anticipated pattern of decreases in the incidence of deficiencies as incomes rise. Not anticipated, however, is the consistency of the pattern across household types. For husband-wife renters, who on average are clearly in a superior economic position compared to other renters, the incidence of plumbing, kitchen, and maintenance deficiencies for the group in poverty is several times higher when compared to the incidence for those with incomes between poverty and twice the poverty level. Impoverished singles and "other" households live in deficient units at similar rates.

Another approach to thinking about the number of householders living in deficient dwellings is to consider only that subset of dwellings that have persistently exhibited deficiencies over time. To address the rate-of-deficiencies issue in this way, we draw on recent work done at The Urban Institute using the 1974–1978 Annual Housing Survey data. As noted, this survey returns to the same dwellings every year, as long as the unit remains in the housing inventory. Thus, it was possible to observe the permanence of various deficiencies.

The definition of deficiencies used as the starting point in this analysis—the HUD/Simonson definition—differs substantially from that described earlier in the chapter.[3] Rather than review the new definition in detail, it is more efficient to describe the general way in which it was modified to measure permanent deficiencies and then give the resulting final definition.

To determine which dwellings were permanently deficient, the deficiencies of each unit (as defined by HUD/Simonson) for each year 1974 to 1978 were examined. A major consideration was the year-to-year persistence of deficiencies because highly volatile patterns of deficiencies—say, deficient every other year—point to two problems. First, volatility may indicate measurement problems, rather than "true" variation, that is, the household perceives a deficiency this year but not the next, or the same condition is perceived differently by successive households occupying the unit. Second, while the condition is accurately measured, correcting it is a routine task and may be so small that it is done fairly frequently. Such deficiencies may therefore not be sufficiently serious to classify a unit as permanently deficient.

As a measure of the stability with which each deficiency occurred, we calculated the fraction of housing units reported to have a particular deficiency that had the deficiency in any two (or more) consecutive years over the five-year period from 1974 to 1978. For each deficiency included in the HUD definition, this rate was calculated as the following fraction:

$$\frac{\text{Housing Units with Deficiency X in at least two consecutive years, 1974 to 1978}}{\text{All Housing Units with Deficiency X, 1974 to 1978}}$$

It was desirable to exclude housing problems affecting only a small fraction of these dwellings because of the likely reporting problems, the evanescent nature of the deficiency, and the likelihood that small proportions would fall within the bounds of sampling or nonsampling error. Therefore, the arbitrary guideline was adopted that at least one-third of the housing units reporting the presence of a particular deficiency at any time over the study period had to have that deficiency present in at least two consecutive years.

All deficiencies that met the above criterion of persistence in at least two consecutive years constituted the population of deficiencies from which the persistence measure was then developed; those are listed in table 2-11. Dwellings that were reported to have any of these deficiencies in at least three of the five years, 1974 to 1978, were considered to be persistently deficient. Under this criterion, dwellings that had a different deficiency in each of three years were considered permanently deficient, as were those that had a particular deficiency in three or more years.

A summary of the incidence of persistent deficiencies is given in table 2-12; deficiencies are for the 1974 to 1978 period, and household characteristics are for 1978. The results differ from those found when examining current deficiencies. For one thing, the incidence of deficiencies is generally less sensitive to variations in current income, within each tenure, location, and age of household level group. This may reflect the greater importance of permanent and long-term income in determining persistent housing deficiencies. A second difference from earlier findings is the similarity of deficiency rates among different tenure and age groups by location: owners and renters, elderly and nonelderly, have broadly consistent deficiency rates in urban areas on the one hand, and in rural areas on the other. The main consistency with prior results is that households in rural areas (shown in the table) and blacks (not shown here) have sharply higher rates of dwelling deficiencies than other households.

The reasons for the different patterns among households in the incidence of current and permanent dwelling deficiencies has yet to be adequately

TABLE 2-11
DEFICIENCIES WHICH CAUSE A HOUSING UNIT TO BE JUDGED PERMANENTLY PHYSICALLY INADEQUATE[a]

Type of Deficiency	*Description of Deficiency*
Plumbing	*Lacks or shares some or all plumbing facilities.* The unit must have hot and cold piped water, a flush toilet, and a bathtub or shower—all inside the structure and for exclusive use of the unit.
	Lacks adequate provision for sewage disposal. The unit must be connected with a public sewer, septic tank, cesspool, or chemical toilet.
Kitchen	*Lacks or shares some or all kitchen facilities.* The unit must have an installed sink with piped water, a range or cookstove, and a mechanical refrigerator—all inside the structure and for the exclusive use of the unit.
Physical structure	*Leaks in basement.*
Common areas	*No elevator in building,* for units two or more floors from the main building entrance in buildings four or more stories high.
Heating	*Has unvented room heaters which burn oil or gas.* If unit is heated mainly by room heaters burning gas, oil, or kerosene, the heaters must have flue or vent.
Electrical	*Lacks electricity.*
	One or more rooms without a working wall socket.

a. Unit must have at least one of these deficiencies in at least three out of five years to be considered permanently deficient.

explored. At this point we can only note that about 12 percent of elderly urban renters and 40 percent of elderly rural renters live in dwellings that have major defects of some type year after year.

A final dimension of housing quality of particular relevance for the elderly is the extent to which dwellings have been modified to make them more useful for persons with activity limitations or health problems. It is well known that many elderly persons have some problem of this sort. Determining which of these problems is severe enough to mean that dwelling modifications are "needed" has been much more difficult. This determination has been rendered intractable by the episodic nature of some problems and by other

TABLE 2-12
PERCENTAGE OF DWELLINGS CLASSIFIED AS PERSISTENTLY DEFICIENT 1974–1978, BY AGE OF HEAD, TENURE, INCOME, AND LOCATION IN 1978

	Elderly Renters		*Nonelderly Renters*		*Elderly Homeowners*	
Income	*Urban*	*Rural*	*Urban*	*Rural*	*Urban*	*Rural*
less than $5,000	14	43	20	41	18	35
$5,000–$10,000	10	37	13	28	13	27
$10,000–$20,000	13	36	13	26	12	24
over $20,000	14	a	11	29	11	28

SOURCE: Tabulations of data described in Newman, Struyk, Manson (1982).

a. Too few observations to be reliable.

household members adjusting their activities to compensate for the reduced capabilities of one member. In this presentation, we can provide only the barest suggestion of the degree to which dwellings have been modified where necessary. We draw on a recent study done using the 1978 Annual Housing Survey. The 1978 survey instrument was unique in that it contained a battery of questions on the health status and activity limitations of each member of the household and, when any problem was recorded, an inventory was made of special features present in the dwelling.[4]

We focus on those households which report a member having serious activity limitations, such as having difficulty going up and down stairs. In particular, we report the number of such elderly headed households, as well as the share of these households who have any type of special feature in their dwellings, ranging from grab bars to ramps to specially equipped telephones, to bathrooms modified for wheelchair use. There are about 1.7 million households in this group, or a little over 10 percent of elderly households in 1978. These calculations are presented in table 2-13 for five household types. The definition of household type differs somewhat from that used elsewhere in this section to better distinguish the amount of potential within-family assistance available.

The figures show that for every household type homeowners are more likely to live in units with special features than are renters. For no household type, however, do more than one-third of the units have those features. Among different types of households, the lower incidence of special features for husband-wife families that contain additional persons may indicate the importance of personal assistance in substituting for dwelling modifications. On the other hand, the low incidence of these features for elderly men living alone (compared to others in their respective tenure groups) may mean that

TABLE 2-13
COUNT OF ELDERLY HOUSEHOLDS REPORTING A MEMBER WITH ACTIVITY LIMITATIONS AND THE PERCENT OF THOSE HOUSEHOLDS HAVING SPECIAL MODIFICATIONS TO THEIR DWELLINGS[a]

	Renters		*Homeowners*	
	Count of Those With Limitation (100)	*Percent With Unit Modified*	*Count of Those With Limitation (100)*	*Percent With Unit Modified*
Household				
Males living alone	39	13	75	25
Females living alone	228	21	431	33
Husband-wife only	71	14	329	30
Husband-wife with others	29	5	224	14
Other household types	66	17	227	24

SOURCE: Tabulations of 1978 Annual Housing Survey data. For details see Struyk (1982).

a. The activity limitations include trouble going in and out of the unit, getting around the house, going up and down stairs, and needing personal assistance and a mechanical aid to get around the house.

Special features include items ranging from grab bars to special faucets, to a specially equipped kitchen. Presence of any item was sufficient for the unit to be counted in this tabulation.

only the "stronger" men are able to continue living alone. Alternatively, it may signal that elderly men receive more assistance from friends or nonresident family members than others receive.

Housing Expense Burden

What fraction of their incomes must the elderly devote to housing in order to enjoy the standard of housing described? It is an important question, one whose presumed answer—"too much"—has given birth to a series of programs to help the elderly, including locally financed real estate tax relief under so-called circuit breakers and federally financed emergency utility payments.

Before the question can be addressed, the issue of the appropriate standard to be employed must be confronted. Should the same standard apply to the elderly as to other households? What is the relevant absolute standard? Likewise, a whole series of definitional problems must be resolved. These items have been discussed elsewhere and need not detain us.[5] A conservative definition of excessive housing expense—over 35 percent of income going to housing—has been adopted. The definition of out-of-pocket housing expense is quite broad. For both renters and homeowners it includes utilities.

However, the definition excludes maintenance expenditures, which are especially important for owner-occupants. A quite comprehensive income definition is also employed, but it does not encompass imputed rents from owner-occupants living in their own dwellings.

Using these definitions, the central finding is that in 1976 the average household headed by an elderly person devoted only slightly more of its income to housing than did the average nonelderly household—23 percent vs. 20 percent. The reason for the closeness between the two groups is that more of the elderly are homeowners with no mortgage debts on their properties.

The basic information on the share of income devoted to housing by the elderly is summarized in table 2-14. Again, greater detail is provided for renters than for homeowners. Panel A of the table contrasts the situation for renters, and the two groups of homeowners, that is, those with and without mortgages on their properties. The higher share of income going to out-of-pocket expenditures for renters is clear: 38 percent of renters spend over 35 percent of their incomes on housing compared with 10 percent of homeowners without mortgage debt, who constitute 85 percent of all elderly owner-occupants. A greater fraction of elderly renters spend over 35 percent of their income on housing than their nonelderly counterparts: 38 vs. 21 percent.

Still, the most interesting patterns are among the elderly renters themselves. First, those with incomes below the poverty line are spending an extraordinary share of income on housing; 41 percent spend more than 45 percent of income. Twenty-six percent of those with incomes between the poverty line and twice the poverty line devote over 45 percent of income to housing. As seen earlier, being in poverty overlaps heavily with living alone; 43 percent of this group spend more than 35 percent on housing, 28 percent spend more than 45 percent. Husband-wife households have the lowest incidence of excessive expense burdens, that is, spend over 35 percent of income for housing. Only fairly small differences in the incidence of expense burdens of over 35 percent are reported between whites and blacks. This indicates that blacks, while living in substandard housing much more frequently, are devoting less of their more limited incomes to housing. A similar pattern is also evident for metropolitan and nonmetropolitan areas.

Although the data presented in table 2-14 document the housing expense burdens of the elderly, they do not provide much of an idea of the expenditure levels. For example, over half of the poor elderly renters spend over 35 percent of their income on housing, but how much rent do they pay? Expenditures are another measure of housing services consumed and are of interest. Table 2-15 displays the distributions of monthly housing expenditures for the three household types and three income groups used throughout this chapter.

TABLE 2-14
SHARE OF INCOME DEVOTED TO HOUSING
BY THE ELDERLY, 1976
(Percentage)

	Share of Income Spent on Housing			
	.25 or less	*.26 to .35*	*.36 to .45*	*over .45*
A. Tenure groups (elderly)				
Renters	40	22	15	23
Owners without mortgages	80	10	5	5
Owners with mortgages	50	19	12	18
B. Renters				
1. Elderly vs. Nonelderly				
elderly	40	22	15	23
nonelderly	61	16	8	13
2. Household type (elderly)				
husband-wife	48	23	14	15
single persons	36	21	15	28
Others	46	19	16	19
3. Income (elderly)				
in poverty	24	18	16	41
poverty to twice poverty	31	24	18	26
over twice poverty	67	20	9	5
4. Race (elderly)				
black	44	23	16	17
nonblack	40	22	14	23
5. Location (elderly)				
in metro areas	40	21	15	24
outside metro areas	43	23	15	19

SOURCE: Struyk and Soldo (1980), table 3-11.

The bulk of renters spent between \$100 and \$200 per month in 1976, including one-third of those with poverty-level incomes. What is even more striking is the large proportion who spend less than \$100 per month: 47 percent of single persons and over 60 percent of those in poverty. Indeed, 24 percent of the impoverished elderly renters spend less than \$50 per month. There is little doubt that the housing inhabited by those 64,000 households, or the 339,000 single-person renters (of all incomes) who spend the same, is of poor quality.

TABLE 2-15
PERCENTAGE DISTRIBUTION OF MONTHLY HOUSING EXPENSES OF ELDERLY RENTERS: 1976

	Housing Expenses						
	Under 50	*$51- $100*	*$101- $150-*	*$151- $200*	*$201 $250*	*$251- $300*	*Over $300*
Household type							
Husband-wife	2	18	24	24	15	8	8
Single person	14	33	24	17	6	3	2
Other	6	21	28	20	13	5	6
Income status							
Below poverty	24	38	22	11	4	1	1
Poverty to twice poverty	6	33	29	19	8	2	2
Over twice poverty	1	10	20	28	18	11	11

SOURCE: Struyk and Soldo (1980), table 3-12.

These figures, combined with those on expense burden, point to a cruel dilemma on the part of hundreds of thousands of the elderly: either to live in adequate housing and devote a major share of income to this purpose, or to be able to purchase other needed goods and services and spend only minimum amounts on housing. There is a second group in a more desperate situation: those for whom expenditure of only $50 per month represents a burden. This group includes anyone with an annual income of $1,714, or 63 percent of the official poverty-income level in 1976. As the data have shown, the majority of the elderly are neither impoverished nor devoting over 35 percent of their incomes, but a significant number do have very serious income and housing problems.

We now turn to the share of income devoted to utilities, a subject of intense public interest in recent years. Indeed, substantial funds have been appropriated by the Congress to help those who are unable to afford to heat their homes. We rely heavily on the calculations done by Wayne Hoffman using AHS data for those households which paid their own heating utility bills. Table 2-16 gives the essential information for the elderly and nonelderly combined: those households with incomes of less than 75 percent of the poverty line are spending a much greater share of their incomes for energy than even those in the 75–125 percent of poverty income group. Households in the under 75 percent of poverty group in the North Central and South census regions, for example, are spending about 30 percent of their incomes for home energy and about half of this for the fuel used in heating.

TABLE 2-16
PERCENT OF HOUSEHOLD INCOME SPENT ON HOME ENERGY

	Household Income as a Percent of Poverty			
	<75%	*75-125%*	*125-200%*	*>200%*
A. Heating Fuels Only				
Northeast	26	9	5	3
North Central	16	7	4	2
South	14	5	3	1
West	12	4	2	1
B. All Home Energy				
Northeast	41	16	10	5
North Central	29	14	8	4
South	30	13	8	4
West	25	9	5	3

SOURCE: Hoffman (1979), tables 8 and 9.

These basic points are reinforced by the data in table 2-17 which disaggregate the figures on the share of income spent on heating fuels by tenure and by whether or not the head of the household is age 65 or older. Looking only at the heating fuels expenditures is useful for this point because there is a smaller variance in expenditure across income groups for energy used for this purpose than for other household activities.[6] All households with incomes below the poverty line are devoting over 10 percent of their income to heating fuels alone. Among households with incomes of 75 percent of the poverty level or less, homeowners in the two warm regions spend sharply more for heating fuel than do renters in the same areas. For the other income groups, little difference by tenure is observed. As between elderly and nonelderly headed households, no meaningful distinction is apparent, even among the poorest households.

Location. The spatial location of the elderly affects housing policy designed to address their needs in two ways. The type of need may differ by location. We have seen, for example, that the physical inadequacy of dwellings is a much more serious problem in rural than in urban areas. In addition, however, the delivery of assistance may be affected by location. If rural markets were characterized by the absence of an adequate supply of rental units, a program providing rent supplements would have little impact on the quality of housing occupied by recipients. The task in this section is to briefly describe the current location of elderly households.

TABLE 2-17
PERCENT OF HOUSEHOLD INCOME SPENT ON HOME HEATING FUELS BY POVERTY STATUS, TENURE, AND AGE OF HEAD

	Household Income as a Percent of Poverty			
Panels A and B	*<75%*	*75-125%*	*125-200%*	*>200%*
A. Tenure				
Very Cold[a]				
Owners	22	8	5	5
Renters	16	7	5	5
Moderately Cold				
Owners	25	8	5	2
Renters	13	6	4	2
Warm				
Owners	16	6	3	1
Renters	12	5	3	1
Hot				
Owners	11	4	2	1
Renters	11	3	2	1
B. Age of Head of Household				
Very Cold				
Elderly	19	9	6	3
Nonelderly	21	7	4	1
Moderately Cold				
Elderly	20	8	5	3
Nonelderly	19	7	5	2
Warm				
Elderly	13	7	4	2
Nonelderly	15	5	3	1
Hot				
Elderly	10	3	2	1
Nonelderly	12	3	2	1

SOURCE: Hoffman (1979), tables 11 and 13.

a. Region definitions are the same as those used by Goedert et al.

The basic information is provided for 1978 in table 2-18. Seventy-one percent of the elderly live in urban areas. Twenty-nine percent are in rural areas, with only 4 percent on farms. Only about 20 percent of the elderly in urban areas live outside metropolitan areas. Within metropolitan areas, the elderly are about evenly split between central cities and their suburbs. Not surprisingly, the homeownership rate is higher in rural areas. Indeed, only

TABLE 2-18
DISTRIBUTION OF ELDERLY HOUSEHOLDS BETWEEN URBAN AND RURAL AREAS, BY TENURE STATUS IN 1978

A. Distribution of Households Across Locations

	All Households		*Homeowners*		*Renters*	
	Number[a]	*Percent*	*Number*	*Percent*	*Number*	*Percent*
Total	15,775	100	11,217	100	4,558	100
In urban areas						
Total	11,191	71	7,389	66	3,802	83
Inside SMSA	8,778	56	5,627	50	3,151	69
Outside SMSA	2,413	15	1,762	16	651	14
In rural areas						
Total	4,583	29	3,828	34	755	17
Nonfarm	3,985	25	3,276	29	709	16
Farm	600	4	553	5	47	1

B. Distribution of Households by Tenure

	Homeowners	Renters
Total	71	29
In urban areas		
Total	66	34
Inside SMSA	64	36
Outside SMSA	73	27
In rural areas		
Total	84	16
Nonfarm	82	18
Farm	92	8

SOURCE: Tabulations of 1978 Annual Housing Survey data.

a. In thousands.

16 percent of the elderly in rural areas are renters; these renters account for about 5 percent of all elderly households. The incidence of renting is highest in the urban portions of metropolitan areas; but even here the rate is only 36 percent. Nonetheless, elderly renters are heavily concentrated within metropolitan areas; in fact, seven out of ten live in the urban parts of SMSAs.

There is substantial variation in the distribution of the elderly among the four census regions (see table 2-19). The South, which has the largest number

TABLE 2-19
DISTRIBUTION OF ELDERLY HOUSEHOLDS
AMONG CENSUS REGIONS IN 1978

	Number of Households[a]			*Percentage*	
	Total	*Owners*	*Renters*	*Households in region of national total*	*Homeowners of all household*
Northeast	3,621	2,221	1,391	23	61
North Central	4,207	3,117	1,090	27	74
South	5,298	3,976	1,322	34	75
West	2,659	1,904	755	17	72

SOURCE: Tabulations of 1978 Annual Housing Survey Data.

a. In thousands.

of elderly headed households, has twice as many as the West, and it is the home of one-third of all elderly households. The Northeast and North Central regions each account for about one-fourth of all elderly households. The Northeast has a higher incidence of elderly occupying rental housing than the other regions—39 percent versus 25 percent. The other regions all cluster around 25 percent.

These simple tabulations point out that in concentrating assistance to elderly households who are renters, the government will be heavily concentrating its assistance on metropolitan areas. As to regional differentiation, such assistance would be moderately more concentrated in the Northeast than elsewhere. Of course, for this pattern to hold requires that assistance be allocated solely on the basis of the number of elderly renter households present. When housing defects and housing expense burdens are considered as well, a much more diffuse pattern of assistance may emerge.

Mobility

The willingness to move on the part of an elderly person or couple may well make the difference between receiving federal assistance with housing or not. This observation is more obvious for occupancy in the housing projects whose construction the federal government has subsidized; to live there one must shift from his current dwelling. However, it is a factor even in the rental assistance programs such as Section 8 (existing) or vouchers, in which payments are contingent on living in a dwelling that passes certain minimum standards for health and safety. Becoming a recipient may mean relocating if the initially occupied dwelling cannot be economically brought up to standard or the owner of the unit is unwilling to make needed improvements.

Thus, lower propensities to move by the elderly may restrict participation in these programs.

The purpose of this section is to briefly acquaint the reader with the mobility rates of the elderly, again concentrating on elderly renters. Because the base majority of moves are local, we simply examine total mobility levels, not attempting to distinguish between long-distance and local moves. We also ignore regional shifts in the location of the elderly.[7]

A general idea of the mobility of the elderly is provided by the figures in table 2-20. Two widely appreciated facts stand out from these figures. One is that the mobility levels of the elderly are only about one-third of those of the population at large. Inside metropolitan areas, 11 of every 100 homeowners will move in 12 months, but only 4 of 100 elderly homeowners; likewise, 36 of 100 renters will change dwellings, but only 11 of every 100 elderly renters will move. The other fact is that homeowners move at much lower rates than their renter counterparts for both the elderly and nonelderly, an outcome one would anticipate given the higher transaction costs of selling and buying a home.

At the same time, there are a couple of observations that were less anticipated. There is little variance in mobility rates of household types among

TABLE 2-20
PERCENTAGE OF HOUSEHOLDS RELOCATING IN THE PAST TWELVE MONTHS BY AGE OF HEAD, TENURE, AND LOCATION: 1978

Elderly Headed Households	*Inside SMSAs*	*Outside SMSAs*
Homeowners	4	3
Renters	11	13
Total		
2-or-more person households		
husband-wife	14	16
other male head	10	4
other female head	10	7
1-person households		
male	11	22
female	11	12
All Households		
Homeowners	11	11
Renters	36	39

SOURCE: U.S. Bureau of the Census, AHS (1981), table A-1.

renters where large deviations from the average mobility rate are found; the rates are often for small groups, such as male-headed but nonhusband-wife families. Elderly single persons and couples have about the same likelihood of moving over a year's time. A second surprise is that there is little variation in the mobility rates of renters with their incomes (see table 2-21). For example, the mobility rates of renters in the $3,000 to $5,000 income group (in 1973) and those in the $10,000 to $15,000 group are identical.[8] Thus income and household type per se do not have much effect on mobility.

Another point of interest is the shift between tenure status that can occur with relocation: how often do homeowners become renters and vice versa? As shown by the data in table 2-22, the shift is definitely away from owner-occupancy when the elderly relocate. While 61 percent of those who are owner-occupants before moving remain homeowners when they relocate, 39 percent shift to being renters. Lifewise, only 15 percent of those initially

TABLE 2-21

MOVEMENT RATES OF ELDERLY RENTERS BY INCOME CLASS: 1973

Income	*Percent Moving in Last 12 Months*
Under $3,000	13
3,000 to 5,000	16
5,000 to 7,000	12
7,000 to 10,000	14
10,000 to 15,000	16
over $15,000	17
All Groups	14

SOURCE: U.S. Department of Housing and Urban Development (1979).

TABLE 2-22

PERCENTAGE DISTRIBUTION OF RECENTLY MOVING ELDERLY HEADED HOUSEHOLDS BY TENURE IN PREVIOUS AND PRESENT UNITS: 1973

		Owner-occupied		*Renters*	
Previous unit	*Total*	*1 Unit*	*2 or more*	*1 unit*	*2 or more*
Owner-occupied	100	55	6	12	27
Rented	100	11	4	21	65

SOURCE: U.S. Department of Housing and Urban Development (1979).

a. Population restricted to those households with the same head of household in both units.

renting shift to homeownership upon moving. Given the much larger number of homeowners than renters, the flow toward renting among relocating elderly households is clear.[9] Unfortunately, at the moment we have little idea how sensitive the magnitude of this flow is to economic incentives, such as the home equity capital gains forgiveness, or the wide-spread availability of housing assistance for renters. Thus, it is very difficult to gauge the likely number of renting elderly who will be eligible and eager to participate in the housing programs.

Summary

The foregoing discussion, with its thicket of tables and data, has provided a factual background on the current housing and living arrangements of elderly households that will facilitate the presentation of analysis in the later chapters. Throughout, more attention has been devoted to renter households since they are the principal subject of this volume. We have seen that the majority of elderly renters live alone and that most of these are women, a pattern that will be carried into the future. Moreover, renters—both couples and individuals—have lower incomes than their homeowning counterparts. Examination of alternative income trajectories for elderly couples and individuals strongly suggests that individuals will lose ground economically compared to couples between now and 1990. As a group, then, renters will be in relatively declining circumstances compared to homeowners, assuming no radical shifts in tenure status.

Overall, the elderly live in units that could be characterized as somewhat smaller and more modest than those occupied by the nonelderly. Three subgroups of the elderly have been identified who have high rates of deficiencies in their units—deficiencies serious enough to prevent the unit from qualifying under Section 8 program standards currently employed by the Department of Housing and Urban Development without incurring significant costs. Very high deficiency rates are experienced by the black elderly, by those living in rural areas, and by the impoverished elderly. For blacks, these rates are shockingly high. For example, in 1976, 162,000 of the 1.2 million elderly black households were living in units without complete plumbing facilities. Poverty status consistently predicts higher rates of such deficiencies for all household types and for both homeowners and renters.

There are a large number of elderly-occupied units with one or more of the six defects examined in this analysis. About 388,000 renters and 303,000 homeowners in 1976 lived in units with one defect, and half as many of each tenure group live in dwellings with two or more. In total, 1.04 million elderly households live in such units—6 percent of homeowners and 15 percent of renters.

The defects of the dwellings over the period from 1974 to 1978 which were occupied by an elderly-headed household in 1978 were also examined. These computations show that about 13 percent of urban renters and 40 percent of rural renters inhabit units with persistent deficiencies. Comparable rates are experienced by urban homeowners but somewhat lower rates by rural homeowners.

The average elderly household spent 23 percent of its income for out-of-pocket housing expenses in 1976, while the average nonelderly household spent 20 percent. It is important to distinguish among three tenure situations: renters, owners without mortgages, and owners with mortgages. The elderly spend a greater share of income on housing for all three groups, but they are much more heavily concentrated in the group with the lowest average expenditures—owners without mortgages—which keeps the overall difference between the elderly and nonelderly modest. There are about 2.3 million elderly households (or 22 percent of the total for whom the census has the necessary information) spending over 35 percent of their incomes on housing—an excessive burden. Again tenure differences are important: 38 percent of renters, 30 percent of owners with mortgages, and only 10 percent of owners with no mortgage debt. Renters with incomes below the poverty line spend an extraordinarily high share of income on housing: 41 percent of such households spend over 45 percent of their income. Interestingly, the differences in housing expense-to-income ratios associated with race and living in rural areas are insignificant; this contrasts sharply with the quality differences observed earlier.

As one might well expect, elderly renters are highly concentrated in urban areas—71 percent of all elderly households live in urban areas but 83 percent of renters. In urban areas one elderly household in three is a renter; in rural areas the rate is one in six. Thus, assisting elderly renters means focusing on urban areas, even though those renters with the greatest housing quality problems live in rural areas. Regionally, there are more renter households in the Northeast and South census regions, with the renter rate being higher in the Northeast than in the other regions.

Finally, we observed that the mobility rates of the elderly are only about one-third of those of the nonelderly, with little variation among renters by income level or household type. These low mobility rates may be found to inhibit participation in housing assistance programs when relocation is necessary to qualify for assistance, a problem which is addressed later in this study.

Chapter 3

ELDERLY PARTICIPATION IN CURRENT PROGRAMS

The previous chapter discussed the general housing conditions of the elderly in the aggregate, as well as types of elderly-headed households who appear to be in the greatest need of assistance. Before we proceed to examine how Reagan administration policies will affect the elderly, the baseline of support provided by the system of housing assistance programs formerly in place will be documented as a point of departure.[1]

Unfortunately, program statistics on the characteristics of households being assisted are not always of the quality they should be. While in some cases well-designed surveys with random samples of participants are available for making the proper inferences about the total participating population, this type of data does not exist for every program. In some instances we must rely on program data submitted by public housing agencies to HUD. The limitation of such data is that not all agencies systematically submit their forms to HUD, and when they do, they do not always provide all of the necessary information required for analysis.

Another problem, as we shall see, is that there is a danger of double-counting and therefore overestimating the true number of households served. This is because the total housing benefits of some assisted families come from two programs; typically one is a supply-side subsidy (such as a direct loan to developers or a reduced interest rate) and the other further compensates for the low incomes of tenants with a rent supplement payment. In this description of pre-Reagan housing assistance, we avoid such double-counting as much as possible.[2]

As noted earlier, elderly participation in HUD assistance programs constitutes only a fraction of the households eligible for those programs; it is important to know to what extent the characteristics of the participating households differ from those of all eligibles. Since one of the major changes made by 1981 legislation was in defining the eligible population, we reserve discussion on the characteristics of the eligibles until chapter 4, where comparisons are made between eligibles under the old rules, and those under the new.

This chapter first describes the major federal rental programs, relating where appropriate, developments in the Carter administration that foreshadow the changes analyzed later. Next, the chapter discusses who it is these programs are meant to serve. This is followed by a more detailed look at elderly participation, including the extent to which the elderly are served by various programs and the types of elderly households that receive assistance.

Public Housing

The oldest and largest federally supported housing program, begun in 1937, is low-rent public housing. By the end of fiscal year 1980, there were about 1.2 million federally supported units of public housing. When it began, the public housing program was intended to meet such anti-Depression objectives as generating employment and eliminating slums. Its present mission is almost exclusively to assist poor households to live in adequate housing.

Public housing is owned and operated by local housing authorities, which are usually distinct from municipal governments. The federal government provides the development costs for constructing the units and now pays a portion of the operating expenses. Local authorities meet the remainder of their operating costs out of rents and utility charges collected from tenants. In order for HUD to agree to provide funds for project development, however, the municipality must sign an agreement to provide certain types of services for the projects and to refrain from levying taxes upon the property. In exchange for assistance, municipalities have generally exercised careful control over where public housing projects are located. The local housing authority, however, has all of the management responsibilities for developing, operating, and maintaining projects.

The authority must operate within the constraints imposed by HUD regulations, both financial and regulatory. HUD rules apply to such areas as accounting procedures, tenant admission and eviction policies, and rent setting. In addition, Congress establishes broad policies for public housing through appropriation levels, through amendments to the initial statute and through its intent as announced in reports accompanying actual legislation. Beginning in 1979, Congress explicitly monitors changes in the regulations that HUD promulgates to implement such legislation.

As the Reagan administration was assuming office, the public housing program, especially in the largest cities, was clearly in trouble. The Carter administration had undertaken several major initiatives to upgrade public housing projects that were "badly distressed." But it was evident that the general way in which projects were funded required reexamination. Although public housing was initially structured so that the only subsidy was for development of the project, changes in the 1960s and 1970s in tenant composition and restrictions on local authorities as to how much rent they could charge (the Brooke amendments restricted this to 25 percent of household income) made it impossible for many authorities to meet their operating costs.

After several years of ad hoc approaches to providing authorities with operating subsidies, HUD developed a "Performance Funding System," which was intended to make the subsidies equitable and yet provide incentives for good management. There are important shortcomings in this system, including the fact that operating funding and subsidies for the modernization of aging projects are on two different tracks, probably resulting in deferred maintenance by some authorities.[3] The more general problem, however, and the one most directly relevant to this discussion, is that the growth of operating subsidies accelerated during the Carter administration, suggesting to some that tenants ought to pay a larger share of these costs through their rent contributions. (In the next chapter, we will deal with the 1981 legislative response to this issue, and its likely impact on the elderly.)

In the largest cities, public housing typically constitutes between 5 and 8 percent of the entire rental housing stock. As table 3-1 shows, cities like Atlanta and Baltimore have percentages exceeding ten. Even were no additional public housing built (which appears to be part of the Reagan administration's overall plan) these figures indicate that such units already comprise a significant proportion of the current rental stock from which low-income tenants choose their dwellings. Below, we will examine figures on the percentage of such units occupied by the elderly.

Section 8

The Section 8 program was enacted as a part of the landmark Housing and Community Development Act of 1974. It actually consists of four distinct elements, Existing, Moderate Rehabilitation, Substantial Rehabilitation, and New Construction.[4] Since Moderate Rehabilitation is administered with the Existing portion of the program, and since only a modest number of units are involved, it is not considered in detail here. Similarly, since Substantial Rehabilitation follows many of the same rules as New Construction, the discussion of these two segments can be combined.

The intent of the 1974 law was to allow local governments the flexibility to provide housing assistance consistent with local market conditions, using

TABLE 3-1
RELATIVE SIZE OF PUBLIC HOUSING IN SELECTED CITIES

	Public Housing as a Percentage of	
City	*All Rental Units*	*All Housing Units*
New York	5.6	4.1
Chicago	5.4	3.4
Los Angeles	1.1	0.6
Philadelphia	9.0	0.4
Detroit	5.0	2.0
Houston	0.9	0.5
Baltimore	10.3	5.6
Indianapolis	2.3	1.0
Washington, D.C.	5.9	4.1
San Francisco	2.4	1.5
Cleveland	8.6	4.6
Boston	8.0	5.7
St. Louis	5.9	3.2
Seattle	5.4	2.5
Denver	4.5	2.3
Atlanta	14.6	8.7
Buffalo	5.8	3.0

SOURCE: Struyk (1980a), table 2.

these and other programs. In a very tight market, with little prospect of the private market relieving the pressure of low vacancy rates, the city could choose a strategy favoring new construction. Where opposite conditions prevail, the city could choose to rely more on the existing stock.

By the end of fiscal year 1980, the Section 8 program, in the aggregate, was nearly as large as the public housing program with approximately 1.1 million units occupied. The element accounting for the most units—over 70 percent—was Section 8 Existing, which assists households in leasing units that meet certain physical standards from the existing, privately owned housing stock.[5] Here, the government pays the landlord the difference between the actual market rent of a unit (up to a HUD-determined maximum called the "fair market rent" for the area) and the rental contribution of the tenant. Since the start of the program, this was calculated at 25 percent of the household's adjusted income, until the law was changed in 1981 to raise this percentage gradually to 30 percent.

Section 8 Existing, unlike public housing, offers participating households substantial freedom in choosing their own units. Once a household applies and is found to be eligible by virtue of its income and household composition, it may elect to stay in its own unit or find another one, provided the unit it selects meets the housing quality requirements, the rent limitation cited above, and is within the administering agency's jurisdiction. In general, approximately half of the program's participants have stayed in their pre-program dwelling, often requiring that repairs be made to their units to bring them up to standard.

Under Section 8, landlords actually receive two separate rent payments. One is the subsidy payment from the public housing agency (PHA) that administers the program and the other is the household's share, paid directly by the participating tenant. As we shall see below, this set of procedures is only one of a number of possible ways a program of "existing" housing might be designed. Some designs involve more governmental responsibility for locating units (such as in the Section 23 program, initiated in 1965 and currently being converted to Section 8) while others, such as the administration's proposal, involve even greater freedom of choice to participating households.[6] Furthermore, the exact specifications for determining how a household's subsidy under a program such as this is calculated can have a profound effect on elderly participation, as we shall see later.

Unlike the Existing segment, the New Construction/Substantial Rehabilitation segment of Section 8 provides a guaranteed rental stream to developers who build or rehabilitate units under the program. In these elements, the HUD area office—or sometimes a state housing finance agency—advertises the availability of funds for building or rehabilitating units in a jurisdiction and developers respond with proposals. If a proposal is acceptable, HUD signs a 20- or 30-year annual contributions contract with that developer, obligating HUD to pay the difference between a tenant's rental contribution and the full rent for the units in the project. These rents are also controlled by a separate schedule of maximum "fair market rents" for newly constructed or substantially rehabilitated units in the area; this schedule is higher, in general, than the one used in the Section 8 Existing segment.

Developers in the program obtain mortgage financing from a private bank, from HUD through the Government National Mortgage Association, or from a state or local agency which raises funds by selling tax-exempt bonds. HUD, through the Federal Housing Administration, generally insures the mortgage.[7]

As the days of the Carter administration were coming to a close, probably the most important issue regarding Section 8 was the increasing cost to the government of newly constructed units. The "fair market rent" schedule for new and substantially rehabilitated units is higher than it is for units from the existing stock because the latter typically need only small repairs and sometimes none at all to qualify for the program. Furthermore, the commitment of the government to subsidize the rental stream involves a much longer segment of future time for the Section 8 segments dealing with new construction and substantial rehabilitation. By Fiscal Year 1981 the long-term commitment of federal assistance for one new unit averaged about $160,000.[8] Some observers, including those in the Office of Management and Budget under the Reagan administration, felt that this subsidy was too "deep" per household, and that more households could be served with greater reliance on the existing segment of Section 8.

Thus, when the Section 8 program is discussed, it is very important to distinguish among its various elements. Section 8 Existing is a fundamentally different program from Section 8 New Construction/Substantial Rehabilitation. The latter is the latest in the federal government's "supply-side" programs; the former is the most recent of the "demand-side" housing programs.

Section 202

The Section 202 program was created by the Housing Act of 1959, but has been changed frequently since then. In several key respects, however, it is unique among the federal programs which have subsidized new construction. First, the program is restricted to serving the elderly and the nonelderly handicapped. Second, the program relies exclusively on nonprofit sponsors to develop and operate projects. Third, the projects are financed by a direct loan to the sponsor (unlike the Section 8 New Construction program), which relieves the sponsor of the need to seek out private financing. Section 202 projects are expected to provide more than shelter, although there are sharp limits on the health care facilities and services to be provided in each project.

Initially, the program provided loans at 0.5 percent interest above the U.S. Treasury borrowing rate. Later, it was modified to provide loans at 3 percent interest, and the sponsors were responsible for all operating expenses. Because it was felt that too many low-income households were excluded due to rent levels which they could not afford, two changes were made in 1974: the applicable interest rate was defined as the U.S. Treasury's long-term borrowing rate; and a Section 8 subsidy was set aside for each unit built under the Section 202 program to insure that at least 20 percent of participants were lower-income households. Thus, since 1974, we have had a Section 202/8 program which combines features of both. Now, most Section 202 projects also receive some Section 8 subsidies.[9]

Overall the Section 202 program has accounted for only a fraction of units under all of HUD's programs. By the end of 1980, an estimated 50,000 units were occupied.[10] When compared to the 1.2 million public housing and 1.1 million Section 8 units, this total is clearly very modest.

Despite its lower volume, the program has been a persistently popular one and is the only new construction program to survive the Reagan administration cutbacks. Thus, it represents a departure from the general policy thrust of relying more heavily on units from the existing stock. Unfortunately, no adequate data are available on the types of households that are being served by the program, particularly since the 1974 changes in the law. Theoretically, at least, these changes should have resulted in an increase in the proportion of poorer elderly households being served.

Section 236 and Other Programs

Several other programs in the aggregate continued to assist about three quarters of a million households but were being phased out even before the Reagan administration came into office. Suspended in the Nixon housing moratorium of 1973, the Section 236 program deserves particular mention because it remains a sizable program through the funding of bona fide commitments issued before the moratorium and by virtue of amendments to existing contracts. In 1980, the program included over half a million units.

Section 236 was created by the Housing Act of 1968. The program provided subsidies to reduce the interest rate paid by mortgagors for multifamily housing projects and, in turn, reduced rents to tenants. The mortgages were also insured by HUD. The program included new or substantially rehabilitated rental or cooperative units for lower income households. Since the beginning, HUD has been able on a selective basis to pay the difference between the tenant's contribution and actual operating costs for a limited number of projects, first through the Rent Supplement program and later through Section 8. Often these additional subsidies have been provided to financially distressed projects to help their owners from going into default on a HUD-insured mortgage. In Section 8, units receiving such subsidies do so under the "Loan Management." Thus, some households in the Section 236 program could just as well be considered as a part of the Section 8 program. One estimate is that about 42 percent of Section 236 units also get a Section 8 subsidy on behalf of the households in the program.[11]

In addition, there are several other programs which continue to serve renter households. All of these are currently inactive, in the sense that they are not being expanded and were not being expanded even before the Reagan administration took office. For example, Section 231, most active in the early 1960s, was a mortgage insurance program designed to offer the frail but mobile elderly an alternative to nursing homes and hospitalization. By 1980, about 65,000 units were insured under this program. Also, Section 221(d)(3), a below market interest rate program for new construction, continued to serve about 50,000 households. We present aggregate figures for these programs, but do not analyze them in detail.

With the exception of Section 202 (which itself is small in scale) the story of the federal government's housing programs in the several years prior to 1981 can be told in terms of Section 8, which grew rapidly in the late 1970s, and public housing, which comprised a large number of units, most of them built in the 1950s and 1960s.

Table 3-2 gives an overview of HUD-subsidized rental programs, with the estimated number of occupied units in each program at the end of 1980. It should be stressed that these are estimates only, because strictly reliable data are unavailable. As the table indicates, over 3.1 million households are estimated to have been served, with the largest number, 1.2 million, through the public housing program. All segments of Section 8 accounted for another 1.1 million, mostly through the Section 8 Existing program. The balance is made up of other, smaller programs.

The table also estimates the number of units in each program which were occupied by elderly heads of households. About 1.2 million or 39 percent of

TABLE 3-2
ESTIMATED OCCUPANCY BY THE ELDERLY IN HUD-SUBSIDIZED RENTAL PROGRAMS, END OF 1980

Housing Program	*Total Units (thousands)*	*Elderly Occupied Units (thousands)*	*Percentage Elderly Occupied*
Public Housing	1,192	443	37.2
Section 8			
Existing	588	195	33.1
New Construction	242	164	67.9
Substantial Rehabilitation	35	18	50.0
Loan Management	288	124	43.1
Section 236	538	222	41.2
Rent Supplements	165	22	13.1
Section 221(d)(3)	50	5	10.0
Section 202	50	40	80.0
Total	3,148	1,233	39.2

SOURCES: U.S. Department of Housing and Urban Development, *FY 1982 Budget* (Revised), March 1981; Paul Burke(1981); 1979 Tenant Income Survey (The Urban Institute); and statistics provided by HUD staff from the Management Information System. Figures on Section 8 exclude Section 202/8 program. Figures on Section 236 exclude units from Section 8 Loan Management and Rent Supplements program. Figures on Rent Supplements exclude units that receive a Section 236 subsidy.

all units assisted were elderly occupied. Again, it was public housing which served the largest number of elderly headed households, about a third of all elderly assisted units. Within individual programs, it is not surprising that such a large percentage of Section 202 households were elderly, given how the program was designed. But about two-thirds of Section 8 New Construction households were also headed by the elderly, as were about half of the Section 8 Substantial Rehabilitation units.

Rent Supplements (when not combined with another subsidy) and Section 221(d)(3) are small and thus do not contribute substantially to the overall picture. Among the sizable programs, the 33 percent of the elderly served by Section 8 Existing deserves particular attention because the Reagan administration proposal involves more reliance on a modified version of this program. Despite the complexities involved in discussing Section 8 Existing's role in the overall system of housing assistance in place in 1980, it can be safely said that the elderly participated at a lower rate in the Section 8 Existing program than in programs using new construction or substantial rehabilitation, either through subsidizing developers in the private sector or through public housing.

This general picture of elderly assistance should not be overstated, however. In one sense, comparing an "existing" housing program with new construction programs which allow for the development of projects especially for the elderly is inappropriate. In both public housing and Section 8 New Construction, program funds can be used for such projects, while Section 8 Existing is not project-based. A more appropriate comparison would be between Section 8 Existing and a new construction program which is unearmarked to serve particular groups through individual projects; such a program does not exist, however.

Whom Were the Programs Intended to Serve?

Before looking more precisely at the profiles of the elderly served by housing assistance programs, it is important to step back and put such information into context by asking whom the HUD renter programs are intended to serve. The actual profile of recipients, in terms of age of head and other characteristics, can be thought of as the result of two general types of factors.

The first are "input" factors, such as legislation, regulations, and program definitions. An obvious rule of interest, for example, is the definition of the eligible family unit. Other regulations also determine which households are being served, such as assets tests, which for some government programs permit higher levels of assets for the elderly than for the nonelderly.[12] Nonelderly households with high levels of assets will be excluded from such programs, and the net result may be to favor elderly participation. Likewise, requiring recertification of income on an annual basis for other households but only every two years for the elderly (as the law specified for HUD programs prior to 1981), favors longer participation by the elderly in such programs.

Beyond regulations, however, it is clear that the actual implementation of programs will result in greater participation by some groups than others. As an example, program "outreach"—how the eligible population is informed about a program—affects participation by household type. Reliance on social service networks for referrals of households to the program probably puts the "working poor" at a disadvantage, because they are not tied into the welfare information network.[13] Although a general marketing plan for new projects must be approved by HUD, outreach is generally left up to local public housing agencies. Hence, there is likely to be wide variation in how outreach procedures determine the recipient profile across communities.

Such input factors are within the control of policy makers and program administrators. The nonprogram factors are less controllable. Market forces and local acceptance, for example, determine in large part what types of new construction of housing is undertaken; and program design is only one set of incentives affecting private developers. Since all of the programs discussed above, with the exception of public housing, rely on private developers and landlords, recipient profiles are heavily influenced by the actions (or inactions) of such individuals. Landlord cooperation, for example, is an important ingredient in the success of the Section 8 Existing program.

Finally, the preferences and perceived needs by the households themselves determine who is served and who is not served. Some households, for example, shy away from government programs because of the welfare image associated with them. Others might reject living in a project or facing the "forced consumption" of more housing than they would otherwise consume, which can accompany a program that requires a housing unit to meet some minimal level of physical standards.[14]

Here we consider the primary input factors in the form of legislation and regulations that pertain to those who are to be served. Only the two major programs, public housing and Section 8, are considered in detail. The most striking aspect of these programs (and HUD rental programs in general) is that once eligible family units are defined, the criteria for eligibility are based on financial circumstances of the household. In general, HUD programs are directed at three groups of households: (1) households of more than two persons, headed by either elderly or nonelderly persons; (2) single individuals who are handicapped or disabled; and (3) single individuals who are elderly.

Thus, these rules in fact favor elderly participation since, in general, the elderly do not have to compete for program slots with nonelderly individuals.[15]

Prior to changes in the law in 1981, the income eligibility limits for Section 8 and public housing were handled differently. Section 8 was the simpler of the two, since households were required to have average annual incomes which were below 80 percent of the area median family income, adjusted for household size. In addition, 30 percent of households had to fall below 50 percent of the area median income.

The older program, public housing, has always been characterized by substantial discretion in setting the maximum income a household can have. HUD regulations allowed authorities to set income limits in relation to those established by Congress for the Section 8 program. When these local limits were within 80 or 90 percent of the Section 8 limit (80 percent of the area median), they would be routinely approved. Deviations in either direction would have to be justified in terms of the housing conditions faced by low-income households in the area. A recent study shows that large authorities differ significantly on how they approached the issue of income limits within these guidelines.[16]

Beyond family unit definitions and income limitations, Congress has also established "priorities" for the public housing admissions system. For example, in 1979 Congress provided that Public Housing Authorities should give preference to families occupying substandard housing and to those involuntarily displaced. The law did not specify what these terms meant, however, and HUD never promulgated regulations for implementing the legislative language.

The most widely discussed priority has been the congressional action to foster an economic mix among tenants in public housing projects. This policy was formally enacted by Congress in 1974, based on the rationale that projects would be more easily managed if they could "avoid concentrations of low-income and deprived families with serious social problems."[17] The 1981 legislation, which makes public housing and Section 8 income limits uniform, may well erode the latitude of public housing authorities in this area.

In sum, the intent of HUD renter programs, as specified by the legislation that authorizes them, is to base eligibility chiefly on income status. In some programs, such as Section 202, categories of households such as the elderly and handicapped are designated as intended recipients. The two major programs, Section 8 and public housing, limit participation of nonelderly single persons who are not handicapped or disabled, and in this sense other households have an advantage in competing for program slots. Perhaps more importantly, to the extent that the elderly had lower incomes, they were more likely to be eligible under pre-1981 rules.

Profiles of Assisted Households

To get a more precise reading of the types of elderly served in metropolitan areas under each of the major programs, we depend on three different data sets. Each data set can be said to be representative of participating households in such areas.

Although we cannot be certain that the profile of participants in non-SMSAs are similar to the ones discussed here, it is clear that the three major programs have roughly the same proportion of households that are elderly nationally as are found within SMSAs. Table 3-3 shows the percentage of elderly in the public housing, Section 8 Existing, and Section 8 New Construction programs for all locations compared to those within SMSAs. Only for public housing is the percentage of elderly less within SMSAs than for the nation as a whole.

Public Housing. Table 3-4 provides a detailed profile of the elderly in the public housing program, for SMSAs. These data come from a survey of a stratified random sample of PHAs that was conducted in the summer of 1979. Tenant characteristics came mostly from agency files on individual households.[18] To provide a helpful contrast, table 3-4 also includes the same characteristics of households headed by the nonelderly in the same locations.

With respect to race, the elderly profile shows roughly half of elderly participants as white, 42 percent as black, and the remainder as other minorities. Nonelderly households, in contrast, are three-fourths black in SMSAs. The sex of head, however, does not differ much between elderly and nonelderly headed households. In both cases, about three-fourths of the participating households are headed by women.

On the other hand, family size differs significantly, with a full 78 percent of the elderly households being comprised of single individuals; as one expects, there is much more variance in the household size of nonelderly headed

TABLE 3-3
PERCENTAGE ELDERLY IN THREE MAJOR HUD PROGRAMS, ALL LOCATIONS AND WITHIN SMSAs

	Percent Elderly	
Program	*All Locations*	*Within SMSAs*
Public Housing	37.2	34.8
Section 8 Existing	33.1	33.3
Section 8 New Construction	67.9	79.3

SOURCES: Burke (1981); 1979 Tenant Income Survey (Urban Institute); Wallace, et al. (1981); and Survey of Repair and Maintenance Activity in the Section 8 Existing Program (Granville Corporation).

TABLE 3-4
PROFILE OF ELDERLY AND NONELDERLY PARTICIPANTS IN PUBLIC HOUSING

	Percentage Distribution[a]	
Household Characteristic	*Elderly*	*Nonelderly*
Race of Head		
White	51%	13%
Black	42	75
Hispanic	5	10
Other	3	2
Sex of Head		
Male	28	23
Female	72	77
Household Size		
1	78	20
2	17	21
3–4	3	35
5–6	1	17
7+	(b)	7
Household Composition		
Single, no children	78	20
Single, with children	3	56
Couples, no children	13	7
Couples, with children	1	13
Other	5	4
Major Source of Income		
Earnings	4	36
Social Security	75	7
AFDC	1	42
SSI	13	8
Unemployment Compensation	1	3
Pensions	6	1
Other	(a)	2
Age of Elderly Head		
$62 \leq$ age < 75 years	55	—
75+ years	45	—
Average Annual Income	$3,496	$4,852

SOURCE: Weighted 1979 Tenant Income Survey, SMSAs only (Urban Institute).

a. Percentages do not always add to 100 because of rounding.
b. Less than 0.5 percent.

households. Elderly couples constitute about 14 percent of all elderly served by the public housing program. Interestingly, a full 45 percent of elderly headed households are among the "old-old" (75 years of age or more), probably indicative of many elderly "aging in place" in older public housing projects.

With respect to income, the average annual income of the elderly is only about $3,500, or $1,300 less than the average for nonelderly households. Where does this income come from? The "major source of income" in table 3-4 is defined as the source representing the largest fraction of all household income. Defined in this way, the table shows that three-fourths of elderly headed households in the public housing program depend on Social Security for the greatest part of their income. Another 13 percent depend on the Supplemental Security Income (SSI) program.

The results on major sources of income, however, could contribute to a false conception about what types of elderly are being served in public housing. Table 3-5 shows that there is significant overlap between Social Security and SSI. About a fourth of the elderly receive income from both sources. Typically, a small SSI payment supplements monthly Social Security payments. On the other hand, about three-fifths of the elderly headed households receive Social Security payments without such supplementary checks.

Section 8 Existing. The data for the Section 8 Existing program come from a study of repair and maintenance activity in that program undertaken by the Granville Corporation for HUD.[19] Because this is a cross-sectional survey of Section 8 Existing households in roughly the same time period as the public housing survey used above, it represents a good data set for comparisons between the two programs. Only SMSAs are included in the Section 8 Existing data presented in this table.

As table 3-6 shows, the racial makeup of elderly households is quite different from that found in public housing. Here, 70 percent of the elderly

TABLE 3-5
OVERLAP BETWEEN SOCIAL SECURITY AND SSI,
PUBLIC HOUSING ELDERLY TENANTS

	Number	*Percent*
Neither Social Security nor SSI	12,518	5%
Social Security only	164,313	59
SSI only	27,114	10
Social Security and SSI	73,226	26

SOURCE: 1979 Tenant Income Survey, SMSAs only (Urban Institute).

TABLE 3-6
PROFILE OF ELDERLY AND NONELDERLY PARTICIPANTS
IN SECTION 8 EXISTING

	Percentage Distribution[a]	
Household Characteristics	*Elderly*	*Nonelderly*
Race of Head		
White	70%	35%
Black	27	61
Hispanic	2	4
Other	(b)	(b)
Sex of Head		
Male	25	17
Female	75	83
Household Size		
1	80	16
2	18	33
3–4	1	37
5–6	(b)	12
7+	(b)	2
Household Composition		
Single, no children	80	16
Single, with children	1	66
Couples, no children	16	2
Couples, with children	0	11
Other	3	5
Major Source of Income		
Earnings	1	27
Social Security	75	11
AFDC	0	31
SSI	9	13
Unemployment Compensation	0	1
Pensions	9	2
Other	4	15
Age of Elderly Head		
$62 \leq$ age > 75 years	70	—
75+ years	30	—
Moved to different unit	35	57
Stayed in same unit	65	43
Average Annual Income	$4,118	$4,997

SOURCE: Survey of Repair and Maintenance, Section 8 Existing Program (Granville Corp.).

a. Percentages do not always add to 100 because of rounding.

b. Less than 0.5 percent.

are white (compared to 51 percent in public housing). On the other hand, household composition is amazingly similar, with 75 percent of the elderly headed by women (72 percent in public housing), 80 percent composed of single individuals (78 percent in public housing), and 16 percent couples (14 percent in public housing). Section 8 Existing, then, is serving the same types of elderly households as defined by these variables, although it is serving minority households less well than public housing.

There are other differences as well. The average annual income of Section 8 Existing households is about $600 higher for the elderly than for those in public housing. Still, the elderly in Section 8 Existing are again poorer than the nonelderly in the same program. While a similar percentage (75) depend on Social Security as the major source of income, fewer in Section 8 Existing rely chiefly on the Supplemental Security Income program. And, significantly, a smaller fraction of the elderly served by Section 8 Existing are among the old-old. Only 30 percent fall in this age group, compared to the 45 percent found in public housing.

Because moving is such a critical element in the Section 8 Existing program, the table includes a breakdown on how many of the elderly and nonelderly moved to a different unit under the program. As one would suspect from mobility data cited in chapter 2, the elderly move far less than the nonelderly. Sixty-five percent of elderly headed households stayed in their original unit compared to 43 percent of the nonelderly.

Section 8 New Construction. Finally, we can construct a profile of participating households in the Section 8 New Construction program from data collected as a part of the study of Section 8 benefits conducted by Abt Associates.[20] Table 3-7 provides this information on the same variables used for the other two programs. Recall that, while a higher percentage of program participants are elderly in this program, the program itself is much smaller than the others.

In the New Construction program, the racial makeup of elderly households leans even further in the direction of serving nonminorities. Eighty-nine percent are white, and unlike Section 8 Existing and public housing, the majority of nonelderly households are also white. But it does not follow that household composition varies along with race. The percentage of elderly headed households that are female headed, that consist of single individuals, and that are couples is strikingly similar across all three programs.

Section 8 New Construction, on the other hand, serves a population of households at a higher level of average annual income; the figures shown in table 3-6 are slightly higher than those for Section 8 Existing, but quite a bit higher than for public housing tenants. Moreover, in the new construction

TABLE 3-7
PROFILE OF ELDERLY AND NONELDERLY PARTICIPANTS
IN SECTION 8 NEW CONSTRUCTION

Household Characteristic	*Percentage Distribution*[a] *Elderly*	*Nonelderly*
Race of Head		
White	89%	69%
Black	8	24
Hispanic	1	4
Other	1	31
Sex of Head		
Male	24	36
Female	76	64
Household Size		
1	84	45
2	16	27
3–4	0	23
5–6	0	4
7+	0	2
Household Composition		
Single, no children	84	45
Single, with children	0	29
Couples, no children	15	11
Couples, with children	0	15
Other	1	0
Major Source of Income		
Earnings	3	39
Social Security	84	25
AFDC	0	13
SSI	5	10
Unemployment Compensation	0	1
Pensions	5	3
Other	4	9
Age of Elderly Head		
$62 \leq$ age < 75 years	72	—
75+ years	28	—
Average Annual Income	$4,299	$5,013

SOURCE: New Construction Cross-Section Survey (Abt Associates).

a. Percentages do not always add up to 100 because of rounding.

program, the percentage of elderly households depending on Social Security as their major source of income is about 10 percentage points higher than the figures for the other two programs. Again, roughly three-tenths of the elderly households are 75 years of age or older, a figure very much like that for Section 8 Existing. Only in public housing do the old-old constitute a significantly higher fraction of all elderly recipients.

Summary

We have seen that roughly 1.2 million households headed by elderly persons were assisted through one or another of HUD's renter assistance programs by the end of 1980. The elderly constituted about 39 percent of all assisted households, although there was significant variation in how much individual programs served the elderly. The Section 202 program and Section 8 New Construction, both of which were designed to bring new units into the stock, assisted the elderly at the highest levels. Section 8 Existing had the lowest fraction of assisted households that were headed by the elderly. Overall, about 72 percent of the elderly were being assisted through new construction programs.

All three major programs were amazingly similar in such participant characteristics as sex of head, household composition, and household size. They did differ with respect to race, however. Public housing serves the greatest percentage of elderly blacks, and Section 8 New Construction the least. Section 8 Existing is somewhere in between. With respect to serving the old-old, 45 percent of the elderly in public housing are in this age group, compared to about 30 percent in the other two programs. Average incomes were lower for public housing, and highest for Section 8 New Construction.

Chapter 4

THE IMPACT OF 1981 LEGISLATIVE CHANGES

Legislation enacted in 1981 can be characterized as the first step in modifying the housing assistance system that was documented in the previous chapter. The changes that were supported by the administration and passed by Congress signaled an opening round for the 1980s; and on the surface, at least, one would expect these changes to affect elderly participation. In fact, as we shall see in this chapter, the impact is considerable. It is important to recall that in many areas of program design, statutory provisions either permit the secretary of HUD broad leeway in defining rules, or permit discretion to public housing agencies at the local level. Prior to 1981, as we have seen, local authorities were given considerable latitude in setting income limits for tenant admissions in public housing. It should also be recalled that while income was the basic eligibility factor, income definitions were not uniform across programs.

How can the 1981 changes be characterized? The 1981 legislation did several things.[1] First, rules relating to such areas as rents, income limits, the definition of income, and recertification of household income were made uniform for the Section 8 and Public Housing programs. Second, the amendments attempted to target program benefits more narrowly on the "truly needy" by lowering income eligibility limits. Third, the amendments attempted to reduce the subsidy to individual households and to increase rental revenues for public housing units by increasing the family contribution to rent. Finally, the amendments, and the rules promulgated by HUD to implement them, attempted to standardize areas such as deductions from countable income and the frequency of recertification of income.

A summary of the 1981 amendments is contained in table 4-1. The changes listed here are a combination of those directly specified by the law and the rules promulgated by HUD in instances when Congress permitted the secretary

TABLE 4-1
SUMMARY OF MAJOR CHANGES IN HOUSING AND COMMUNITY DEVELOPMENT AMENDMENTS OF 1981 COVERING BOTH PUBLIC HOUSING AND SECTION 8

Subject Area	*1981 Change*
Income Eligibility Limit	Eligibility restricted to those with incomes that do not exceed 50 percent of area median, rather than 80 percent. Households between 50 and 80 percent eligible for: (a) 10 percent of units available for occupancy and leased before October 1, 1981, and (b) 5 percent of units available after that date.
Definition of Adjusted Income	1) $300 standard deduction for elderly replaces deduction for medical expenses (Section 8) and 10 percent elderly deduction (public housing). 2) Deduction per minor raised from $300 to $400.
Family Contribution to Rent	Beginning in 1982, current participants pay 26 percent of adjusted income, increasing to 30 percent by 1986 and thereafter; under prior law the rule was 25 percent. New participants pay 30 percent upon admission.
Maximum Family Gross Rent	Highest of the following: (a) 30 percent of monthly adjusted income; (b) 10 percent of monthly gross income; (c) maximum amount of welfare-determined housing costs. Replaces Section 8 formula which depended on household size, income, and medical expenses.
Recertification of Income	Annual recertification for all households replaces two-year reexamination policy for the elderly.

SOURCE: *Public Law* 97-35, August 13, 1981, and *Code of Federal Regulations,* 24 CFR Part 813.

of HUD discretion in establishing rules. In the material below, we will look in detail at three areas of change—income limits, deductions, and tenant rents—and where possible, calculate the effect of the changes on the eligible and participating elderly population. Recertification of income on a yearly basis would mean that the elderly are more likely to be declared ineligible, but we have no way of estimating the extent to which this will occur.

Income Eligibility Limits

HUD renter programs are income-conditioned, that is, the size of the subsidy decreases as household income increases. Like most government benefit programs, the size of the subsidy is also conditioned on the size of the household served, as reflected in HUD programs by higher rents for larger units required to properly house families with more members. This combination of rules for income conditioning establishes an implicit income limit in many subsidy programs, because at some income level, the size of the subsidy reduces to zero. Households above that income level are ineligible.

HUD programs have additional income constraints. As we saw in the previous chapter, for the Section 8 program the income limit was set at 80 percent of the area median income prior to 1981. For the public housing program, authorities who used income limits within 80–90 percent of this figure could do so without HUD approval.

The 1981 amendments made Section 8 and public housing uniform with respect to income limits. Now eligibility is restricted to those with incomes not exceeding 50 percent of area median for both programs. The law does permit exceptions for project-based programs, such as public housing and Section 8 New Construction. In such cases, households between 50 and 80 percent of the area median can constitute up to (a) 10 percent of the units available for occupancy before October 1, 1981, and leased thereafter, and (b) 5 percent of units available for occupancy after that date. In other words, households currently receiving assistance whose income falls above 50 percent of the area median will not be suddenly eliminated from the program, although the long-run intent is to serve primarily households with incomes below 50 percent.

Before we look in more detail at what these changes mean for the elderly, several points should be made about this form of targeting. While the intent of serving more needy households may be a meritorious one, use of income limits to accomplish it has its own problems.

One interpretation of the 80 percent income limit is that it was so high it had little real effect on who joined the program, and that it would have to be reduced rather sharply in order for targeting to improve. About two-thirds of the national participant population falls below 50 percent of area median anyway.[2] Still, the remaining third fall above 50 percent and would therefore be ineligible under the new rules. This group of assisted households would be replaced over time by those below 50 percent, and the number is substantial.

A second general observation about the HUD income limits is that, even when the cut-off is shifted from 80 percent to 50 percent of area median, it is about 40 percent higher than the ''poverty'' definition used elsewhere by the federal government. This result is based on the comparison of 50 percent of the national median and the single national poverty standard. The official poverty definition is basically derived from estimates of the cost of a nutritionally adequate diet, multiplied by three to reflect a typical relationship between expenditures for food and other household expenditures.[3]

Why, then, is it not appropriate to limit eligibility by employing the national poverty definition or some equivalent measure? The answer is that the cost of housing varies widely by location and the need for housing assistance should not be based on a single national standard. This is the basic rationale for employing area median incomes rather than a national figure. Combined with fair market rent calculations, also compiled on an area basis, this rule results in a more equitable way of distributing housing assistance geographically.

A major problem posed by the income limit approach, however, and one made more pronounced by lowering the limit to 50 percent, is illustrated in figure 4-1. This figure simplifies matters by holding constant the household size involved and the Fair Market Rent (FMR)—the rent, estimated by HUD, for which a unit meeting the physical standards of the Section 8 program should be available in a local housing market. Line AB shows how the subsidy is scaled to income, decreasing as income increases. At the income level at point B, the subsidy is reduced to zero and all households with incomes above that level would be automatically ineligible (because their calculated subsidy is not positive in value).

Points C and D show the imposition of the 80 and 50 percent of median cutoffs, respectively. In the Section 8 program as it operated before the 1981 amendments, it was clearly the case that point D was to the left of point B, the implicit cut-off, but point C may have been slightly to the left or slightly to the right. The important point is that a "notch" is created by income limits in the benefit schedule. This admits those to the left of the limit into the program but makes those just to the right of the cut-off ineligible. The notch problem for pre-1981 rules (80 percent) is clearly less severe because benefit levels are so low at that range that households may not have wanted to participate anyway. Benefit levels at the 50 percent notch are higher, and if a household slightly to the left of the cut-off had a bit more income, it would lose a substantial amount of benefits. This creates an incentive for households to the right of the cut-off to reduce their countable income (perhaps by underreporting income, working less, or selling assets at below market value) in order to qualify for the program.

Thus, while targeting to the needy may be justified, the income limit device creates problems when income limits and FMRs (discussed in chapter

FIGURE 4-1
INCOME LIMITS AND THE "NOTCH" PROBLEM

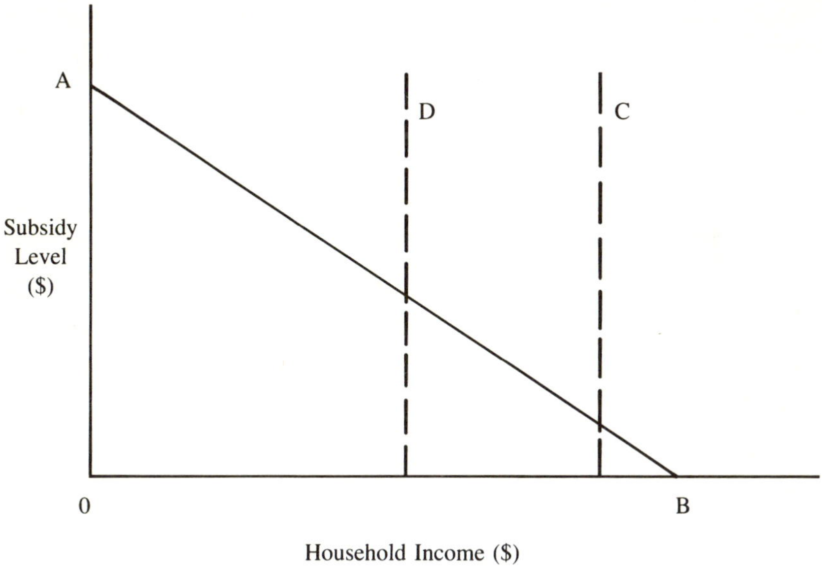

AB = Subsidy Schedule
B = Implicit Cut-off in Schedule
C = 80 Percent of Median Cut-off
D = 50 Percent of Median Cut-off

3) are set separately. Below we shall see how the 50 percent rule translates into numbers of elderly households made ineligible.

One further structural aspect of the income limit merits attention in the context of assistance for the elderly. This is the manner in which HUD adjusts the income limit for various household sizes. Since the 1981 amendments did not change the adjustment procedure, we treat this problem in appendix 1. In short, the result of that analysis shows that by calculating only one area median income for all families, and then adjusting income limits for each household size by a uniform schedule, HUD's adjustment process is biased in favor of one-person households. Since, for the most part, single-person households that are nonelderly and not disabled or handicapped are ineligible for participation, this adjustment process favors single-person elderly households, and will continue to do so under the new income limit.

Impact on Elderly Eligibility. So far the discussion has been at a theoretical level. How many elderly households are involved and how much are the elderly affected as a result of the new rules? First, we address the eligible population. Since these rules were applied after 1981, this section relies on estimates of the 1983 population produced by The Urban Institute's Transfer Income Model (TRIM). This model ''ages'' the population in three stages.

First, the March 1980 Current Population Survey file of households is demographically aged and the number of weeks employed is estimated for each person on the file. Second, TRIM adjusts various sources of income for each household member to incorporate the impact of inflation between the survey year and 1983 (or whichever year is chosen for estimation). Third, TRIM simulates transfer payments for the Aid to Families with Dependent Children program, the Food Stamp program, and the Supplemental Security Income program. The assumptions used to age the population were obtained from the Data Resources, Incorporated, Cyclelong Forecast.[4]

Here, the population of interest is households residing within SMSAs. Table 4-2 shows the effect of imposing the 50 percent of median rule on elderly and nonelderly renter households. It is assumed here that other 1981 amendments were not implemented, in order to observe the separate effect of lowering the income limit. The top section of the table shows the number of renter households in SMSAs. The elderly will constitute 18.2 percent of those households in 1983, according to these projections. If the 80 percent of median rule were in effect, over 70 percent of the elderly renter households, compared to about 45 percent of nonelderly renters, would have been eligible to participate in the major HUD programs.

When the 50 percent rule is applied, we assume here that no exceptions to eligibility are made, as specified in table 4-1. This assumption is required at this point because the data displayed here make no distinction concerning actual program participation; they apply only to income eligibility. Moreover, this assumption is consistent with the overall intent of the 1981 amendments which is to restrict eligibility as much as possible to those below 50 percent of the median.

Table 4-2 shows that the new rule drastically reduces eligibility, from 49 percent of renter households in SMSAs to 29 percent. Both the elderly and the nonelderly suffer drastic reductions in the percent of all households in their age categories that are eligible. The elderly, however, undergo about a one-third reduction while the nonelderly undergo a reduction of about 45 percent. Because the elderly begin with a smaller base of households that are eligible, the shift in the final percentage breakdown of elderly and nonelderly households in the eligible population slightly favors the elderly. Whereas,

TABLE 4-2
EFFECT OF IMPOSITION OF THE 50 PERCENT OF MEDIAN RULE ON INCOME ELIGIBILITY

	Nonelderly Headed Households	*Elderly Headed Households*	*All Households*
All Renter Households in SMSAs			
Number of Households (thousands)	17,449	4,041	21,490
Percent of All Households	81.2	18.2	100.0
Eligible Households Under Prior 80 Percent of Median Rule			
Number of Households (thousands)	7,649	2,860	10,509
Percent of All Households In Age of Head Category	43.8	70.8	48.9
Percent of All Eligible Households	72.8	27.2	100.0
Eligible Households Under 50 Percent of Median Rule			
Number of Households (thousands)	4,190	1,935	6,125
Percent of All Households In Age of Head Category	23.5	47.9	28.5
Percent of All Eligible Households	68.4	31.6	100.0
Percent Change in Eligibility By Imposition of 50 Percent Rule	−45.2	−32.3	−41.7

SOURCE: Urban Institute TRIM Model, for SMSAs only. Figures assume that other 1981 amendments were not implemented, and that 50 percent rule was implemented without exceptions permitted by law.

under the 80 percent rule, 27 percent of eligible households were elderly, 32 percent of eligible households are elderly under the new rule. Thus, the total number of elderly who are eligible is smaller, but the elderly as a proportion of all eligibles is larger.

The logical explanation for the smaller negative effect on the elderly, of course, is that a greater percentage of them fall below the 50 percent of median cut-off than is the case for the nonelderly. This is reflected in lower average incomes under the alternative rules. For the elderly, the average income of eligibles under the old rule was $7,335; under the new rule it is $5,529, about a 25 percent reduction. Figures for the nonelderly show a larger decrease, since more of them were made ineligible.

Besides lower incomes, does the 50 percent rule change the profile of the eligible elderly population? Here we use the same characteristics of elderly households employed in chapter 3, and compare the profiles for the eligible elderly under the two income limit rules. The results appear in table 4-3.

As the table indicates, the race of elderly headed households does not change much, but other characteristics do. Under the new income limit rule, a greater percentage of female-headed households and single-person households are eligible. Formerly, elderly couples constituted about 19 percent of the eligible elderly population; under the new rules they constitute 12 percent. Furthermore, the percentage of eligibles who rely primarily on earnings as the major source of income decreases and the percentages relying on Social Security and SSI increase. There is only a slight change in the percentage of old-old in the eligible population.

Impact on Elderly Participants. So far, we have discussed the effects of the 50 percent income limit on the eligible population. The importance of the eligible population, and its changing makeup, is that it will constitute the pool of households for replacement of current program participants as they leave assistance programs. Thus, the changing profile—more female headed and single person households, for example—will have a similar impact on the profile of all participants.

But prediction of such a direct effect would ignore the fact that not all eligible households have an equal likelihood of participating. Therefore, it is important to observe participants in a more direct way. Here, we examine whether current participants continue or do not continue to be eligible under the new rule. Although the regulations for enforcing the new rule make it clear that the 50 percent limitation will be applied to all new applicants and not to those currently receiving a subsidy, a measure of how many participants remain "eligible" shows the degree to which the participant population will change in the long run. If the income limit is an effective one, large numbers of current participants will be termed "ineligible" by this measure; if not, the limit is not as constraining as it was for defining the eligible population. Furthermore, it is of considerable interest whether or not the particular changes in the eligible population profile we observed above are matched by changes in the makeup of those participating.

Here we use TRIM, employing participation information from the Current Population Survey, which asks (1) whether or not the household lives in public housing; and (2) whether or not the household receives a rent subsidy from the government, excluding public housing. In this analysis we used 1983 overall estimates of the number of households to be assisted within SMSAs, out of the total of 3.8 million assisted households. As in the analysis of

TABLE 4-3

EFFECT OF THE 50 PERCENT OF MEDIAN RULE ON THE PROFILE OF THE ELDERLY INCOME ELIGIBLE POPULATION

Household Characteristic	*Percentage Distributions*[a] 80 Percent Rule	50 Percent Rule
Race of Head		
White	78.3	77.6
Black	14.7	16.0
Hispanic	5.3	4.7
Other	1.7	1.6
Sex of Head		
Male	34.0	28.0
Female	66.0	72.0
Household Size		
1	77.8	85.4
2	19.2	12.0
3-4	2.6	2.3
5+	.3	.3
Household Composition		
Singles	77.8	85.4
Couples	18.9	11.6
Others	3.3	3.1
Major Source of Income		
Earnings	6.9	3.7
Social Security	70.5	77.9
AFDC	4.6	1.1
SSI	8.2	10.7
Unemployment Compensation	.5	.2
Pensions	5.3	4.2
No Income	3.9	2.3
Age of Elderly Head		
$> 62 \geqslant 75$ years	63.7	61.6
75 + years	36.3	38.4
Average Annual Income	$7,335	$5,529

SOURCE: Urban Institute TRIM Model, for SMSAs only.

a. Figures do not always add to 100 because of rounding.

eligibles above, the population of participants was "aged," using the same assumptions about employment, receipt of benefits from other subsidy programs, and the like.[5]

Table 4-4 shows the result of applying the 50 percent rule to 1983 participants. The table shows that, although the impact is smaller than the percentage reduction in the eligible population, it is still very sizable. Were the new rule to be applied retroactively on 1983 participants, 25 percent of the 2.9 million participants in SMSAs would be declared ineligible. In other words, about a fourth of all participants are above the new income limit and would be replaced by those below 50 percent of median. Recall that the shrinkage in the eligible population was around 42 percent.

The table shows that there is a difference in the percentage of elderly and the percentage of nonelderly affected by the rule change. The participating elderly population suffers a 22 percent decline, while the nonelderly undergo a 28 percent reduction. However, because the elderly constitute a smaller fraction of participating households, the overall makeup of the "new" participating population is roughly the same in terms of age of head. This result parallels the result for the eligible population. Whereas the elderly formerly constituted about 40 percent of the participants, they constitute 42 percent under the new rule.

TABLE 4-4

EFFECT OF 50 PERCENT OF MEDIAN RULE ON ELIGIBILITY OF 1983 HOUSING PROGRAM PARTICIPANTS, NONELDERLY AND ELDERLY HEADED HOUSEHOLDS IN SMSAS

	Nonelderly Headed Households	*Elderly Headed Households*	*All Households*
Program Participants Eligible Under 80 Percent Rule			
Number of Participants (thousands)	1,737	1,151	2,888
Percent of all Participants	60.1	39.9	100.0
Program Participants Eligible Under 50 Percent Rule			
Number of Participants (thousands)	1,258	899	2,157
Percent of all Participants	58.3	41.7	100.0
Percent Change in Eligible Participants	−27.6	−21.9	−25.3

SOURCE: Urban Institute TRIM Model, for SMSAs only.

Table 4-5 shows how the population profile for participants differs, once those with incomes above 50 percent of the area median are excluded. The computations here assume that all other rules enacted in 1981 were not implemented, in order to permit examination of the sole impact of the new income limit. Interestingly enough, the changes also parallel to a large degree those in the eligible population. The remaining participants are more likely to be female, and a larger fraction of households consists of single individuals. As expected, the average income declines, with the new figure being about $1,200 less than the average under the old rule. We can conclude that, without any other major program changes beside the income limit reduction, HUD programs would be serving a slightly greater fraction of elderly-headed households. The profile of the population served would match the breakdown in the last column of table 4-5, since this is the population under 50 percent of the area median currently participating and since there is no change in a counter direction in the population of eligibles, from which replacement households would come. The elderly population served would more likely be single individuals and female-headed households.

Standardized Deductions

A second general area of changes brought about in 1981 is that of deductions from income for the purposes of calculating the subsidy that a household shall receive. (Note again that as of the spring of 1982 HUD was still in the process of implementing these legislated changes.) This change applies to the "adjusted income," and not to the annual income figure analyzed above for determination of eligibility.

Changes in the deductions schedule do not affect eligibility directly, although if deductions were dramatically reduced, adjusted incomes would increase in value and the number of eligible households moving beyond the point where the subsidy is still positive in value would increase.

Prior to 1981, Section 8 and public housing rules on deductions were different. In Section 8, three deductions were in force: (a) $300 for each minor; (b) medical expenses exceeding 3 percent of gross income; and (c) unusual expenses, such as amounts paid for child care or for the care of a handicapped or disabled member, where such care was required to enable a family member to be gainfully employed. Note that there was no explicit deduction in the Section 8 program for elderly households as such.

In the public housing program, the deductions rule was more complex and broad discretion was allowed to authorities administering the program. The most important deduction was a standard 5 percent of gross income for nonelderly families and 10 percent for elderly households. Beyond that, there

TABLE 4-5

EFFECT OF 50 PERCENT OF MEDIAN RULE ON PROFILE OF CURRENT ELDERLY HOUSING PROGRAM PARTICIPANTS

	Percent Distribution	
Household Characteristics	*80 Percent Rule*	*50 Percent Rule*
Race of Head		
White	70.0	72.7
Black	22.1	21.9
Hispanic	5.9	14.8
Other	1.9	1.3
Sex of Head		
Male	26.2	23.0
Female	73.7	77.0
Household Size		
1	83.7	87.9
2	13.3	9.2
3-4	3.1	2.9
5+	0	0
Household Composition		
Singles	83.7	87.9
Couples	12.9	8.7
Others	3.4	3.4
Major Source of Income		
Earnings	2.6	1.8
Social Security	71.7	77.7
AFDC	8.0	1.6
SSI	12.2	14.2
Unemployment Compensation	0	0
Pensions	4.5	4.1
No Income	1.0	0.5
Age of Elderly Head		
> 62 ≤ 75 years	63.1	62.6
75+ years	36.9	37.4
Average Annual Income	$6,406	$5,222

SOURCE: Urban Institute TRIM Model, for SMSAs only.

a. Figures do not always add to 100 because of rounding.

were several additional deductions: (a) extraordinary medical expenses exceeding 3 percent of gross income; (b) unusual occupational expenses; (c) child care or care for a handicapped or disabled person necessary to keep a family member employed; (d) $300 for secondary wage earners; and (e) $300 for minors or disabled or handicapped persons. The 10 percent deduction for the elderly was clearly favorable to them when compared to the 5 percent for nonelderly, but the other deductions make the situation much more complex, and the cumulative effect of all the deductions is unclear.

The 1981 amendments established a simpler system for deductions, making them uniform with the Section 8 program. The legislation gave the secretary of HUD broad discretion in specifying the deductions schedule. None of the legislative language indicates any congressional intent to use the deductions mechanism to achieve more targeting, or to give certain types of households an advantage over others. Congress did, however, express the concern that the secretary retain "a deduction related to those child care expenses that are necessary to permit a tenant to be employed."[6] Therefore, in HUD-issued regulations, three deductions are listed: (a) $400 for each minor; (b) $300 for elderly headed households, the disabled or the handicapped; and (c) child care expenses. While the elderly were treated explicitly here, the new rules were clearly intended to offset the elimination of the deduction for medical expenses (assumed to benefit the elderly more) and the 10 percent of income deduction in public housing.

From HUD's point of view, the standard deduction of a fixed dollar amount makes sense because it is administratively simple and is broadly consistent with reforms in other benefit programs. In one site of the Experimental Housing Allowance Program (EHAP), for example, one-third of the clients claimed a deduction for medical expenses exceeding 3 percent of gross household income. Since these expenses are allowable over a one-year period, and since medical expenses involve many small items, the amount of documents to be handled can be enormous.[7]

On the other hand, a standard deduction, by definition, does not account for individual differences in expenditures by households and some equity may therefore be sacrificed. While the new deductions schedule allows for a degree of differential treatment among nonelderly by including a separate child care deduction, no equivalent deduction exists for elderly households. Additionally, fixed dollar amounts mean that the deduction will not change as households' incomes change. The previous 5-10 percent of income deduction in public housing was superior to the current fixed dollar amount in this sense.

Data available to analyze the impact of the new deduction scheme are not detailed enough to assure precise estimates of its worth to participating households. Here we use a gross measure of the percentage of participating households who, when the new deductions are substituted for the old, continue to receive a positive subsidy, absent other program changes. One would expect that more households would remain eligible for a positive subsidy under the new deductions than under the old, if the new deductions are worth more.

Using TRIM projections for the 1983 participating population, table 4-6 shows that this was true for SMSA program participants. However, the effect is exceedingly small. The top panel of the table shows that under the 80 percent income limit, the new deductions rule has an effect that is imperceptible, given the level of precision used in this report. Fewer than .05 percent of all households participating are affected by the new deductions rule. When the high income limit is used, so few households change their eligibility status from a positive to a negative subsidy, that the final numbers (rounded off) remain the same.

TABLE 4-6

IMPACT OF 1981 DEDUCTION RULE ON CONTINUED PARTICIPANT ELIGIBILITY

Income Limit/Deduction Rule	*Nonelderly Headed Households*	*Elderly Headed Households*	*All Households*
80 PERCENT INCOME LIMIT			
Pre-1981 Deductions			
Number of Households (thousands)	1,737	1,151	2,888
Percent of all Participants	60.1	39.9	100.0
1981 Deductions			
Number of Households (thousands)	1,737	1,151	2,888
Percent of all Participants	60.1	39.9	100.0
Percent Change in Eligibility	(a)	(a)	(a)
50 PERCENT INCOME LIMIT			
Pre-1981 Deductions			
Number of Households (thousands)	1,258	899	2,157
Percent of all Participants	58.3	41.7	100.0
1981 Deductions			
Number of Households (thousands)	1,279	899	2,178
Percent of all Participants	58.7	41.2	100.0
Percent Change in Eligibility	+1.7	(a)	(a)

SOURCE: Urban Institute TRIM Model.

a. Less than 0.05 percent.

The bottom panel shows the effect of the new deductions when the 50 percent income limit is imposed on participants. Here the result is also small—less than 1 percent overall—but a bit larger than under the higher income limit. The nonelderly show a slightly higher increase in eligibility than do the elderly, although in neither case are these figures large enough to draw firm conclusions. Furthermore, detailed examination of the types of households affected by the deductions rule change would not be very reliable.

Tenant Rent Contributions

Unlike the area of deductions, Congress was quite explicit when it came to the rents families should pay. Public Law 97-35 reads:

> A family shall pay as rent for a dwelling unit assisted under this Act the highest of the following amounts, rounded to the nearest dollar: (1) 30 per centum of the family's monthly adjusted income; (2) 10 per centum of the family's monthly income; or (3) if the family is receiving payments for welfare assistance from a public agency and a part of such payments, adjusted in accordance with the family's actual housing costs, is specifically designated by such agency to meet the family's housing costs, the portion of such payments which is so designated.

This new rule replaced different rules used in Section 8 and public housing. In Section 8, most households paid 25 percent of adjusted income, although some households could pay less. For example, households with six or more minors falling below 50 percent of the area median were required to pay 15 percent of adjusted income toward rent. Households with eight or more minors, but not below 50 percent of the median could pay 20 percent. In general, these exceptions were directed toward very large families, and therefore were of no benefit to the great majority of elderly.

Section 8's 25 percent rule followed the precedent of the "Brooke Amendments" of 1969–71 for public housing. These amendments established a statutory ceiling of 25 percent of adjusted income on rent charges. One study showed that the 25 percent rule of thumb has been used consistently in this century by mortgage lenders (who expect prospective borrowers who wish to spend more than 25 percent of their income for mortgage payments to be unable to meet those payments) and in housing legislation.[8] As we saw in chapter 2, this ratio does not correspond very well with actual percentages paid by renters, and especially by elderly renters who, on average, pay more than 25 percent.

Using a fixed rent-to-income ratio to calculate how much a family should pay is an unambiguous standard that is administratively simple. However, some argue that the standard should differentiate between households of different incomes, family size, and consumer budget requirements.[9] In fact, such a standard was part of the Section 8 program prior to 1981, as discussed above; it now has been abandoned for the uniform 30 percent rule.

All new participants will be subject to the 30 percent rule upon admission. For current participants, the new rents will be gradually changed upon the first reexamination after January 1, 1982, so that no single annual rent increase will be greater than 10 percent. The following schedule has been adopted for implementing the new rule:

Effective Date of Reexamination	Percentage
January 1 - December 31, 1982	26
January 1 - December 31, 1983	27
January 1 - December 31, 1984	28
January 1 - December 31, 1985	29
January 1, 1986 and thereafter	30

All of these figures, of course, apply to gross rents. In instances where a household pays for utilities, an allowance is deducted.

What impact should we expect the new tenant contribution rate to have? Clearly, it should result in making some current participants ineligible because their own contribution to the rental payment replaces what the government would have contributed in the past. This is illustrated in figure 4-2, which includes a subsidy schedule for the tenant contribution rate of 25 percent (Line AB) and a steeper schedule at 30 percent (Line AE). Those with incomes between zero and E will have their subsidy reduced and will have to pay a greater share on their own. But those with incomes between E and B will now get no subsidy at all. Because we are dealing with an income range that is on the high side, we expect the reduction in eligibility among participants as a result of this rule to be less pronounced than we observed earlier for the income limit reduction.

In fact, TRIM estimates bear out this expectation. Table 4-7 indicates that, overall, the separate influence of the 30 percent tenant contribution rule is to reduce eligible participants by about 11 percent. Interestingly enough, there is no substantial difference between elderly and nonelderly households in this regard, unlike the impact observed earlier that resulted from the income limit reduction. The small change is in the direction of favoring the nonelderly, but the resulting participant population breakdown changes hardly at all.

Summary: The Combined Impact

Each of the major 1981 legislative changes has been considered here for its impact on the elderly population. The new eligible population was defined by a major change—reducing the income limit from 80 percent of the area median to 50 percent. The participating population for future admissions was

FIGURE 4-2
ALTERNATIVE TENANT CONTRIBUTION RATES

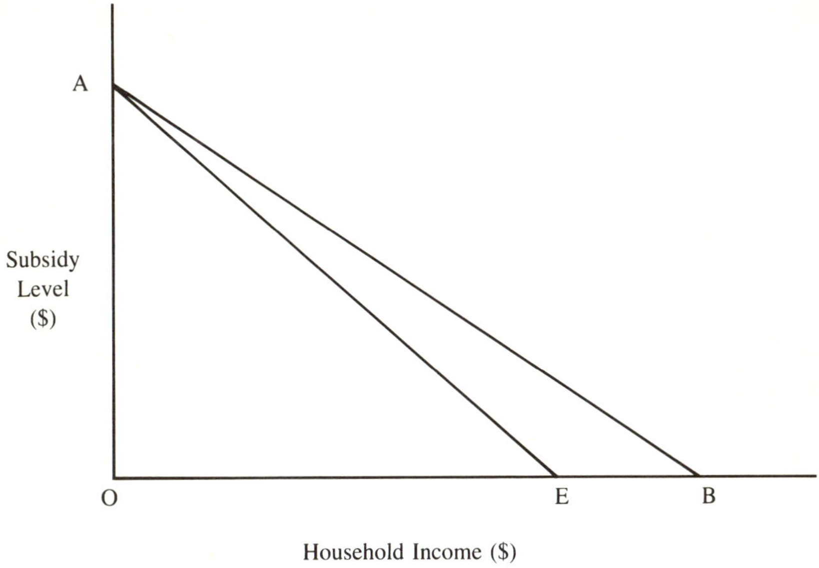

AB = Subsidy Schedule, 25 Percent Tenant Contribution Rule

AE = Subsidy Schedule, 30 Percent Tenant Contribution Rule

changed by the new income limit, standardizing deductions, and increasing the fraction of income tenants must pay toward rent.

Table 4-8 summarizes the estimates for the impact of these changes. With respect to the eligible population, a full 42 percent reduction is evident for all SMSA households; the elderly are less likely to be eliminated from the pool of eligibles as a result of 1981 legislative changes. Because the elderly constitute a smaller percentage of eligible households overall, the percentage distribution in the new eligible pool changes by a lesser amount. Nevertheless, the elderly increase their fraction of the eligibles from 27 percent to 32 percent.

The bottom panel shows the effects on the eligibility of current participants. Although rules will not be implemented which would suddenly eliminate current participants who are no longer eligible, these figures indicate

TABLE 4-7
EFFECT OF 30 PERCENT TENANT CONTRIBUTION RATE ON ELIGIBILITY OF PARTICIPANTS

	Nonelderly Headed Households	*Elderly Headed Households*	*All Households*
Participants Under 25 Percent Tenant Contribution Rule			
Number of Participants (thousands)	1,737	1,151	2,888
Percent of all Participants	60.1	39.9	100.0
Participants Eligible Under 30 Percent Tenant Contribution Rule			
Number of Participants	1,542	1,021	2,565
Percent of all Participants	60.2	39.8	100.0
Percent Change in Eligible Participants	−11.2	−11.3	−11.2

SOURCE: Urban Institute TRIM Model.

the likely nature of the future replacement process, as households drop out. Each of the rules had a different impact. The largest impact is observed for the new income limit, with a six point spread between the effects felt by the elderly and those felt by the nonelderly. Standardized deductions made little difference on their own. The 30 percent tenant contribution rate had about the same impact on the elderly and the nonelderly, in the area of 11 percent.

All rules combined should be expected to be less than the impact of these separate rules added together, because some households are eliminated for more than one reason and should not be counted more than once. The table demonstrates this result, with an overall reduction of about 31 percent. The elderly participants do better than the nonelderly by about 8 percentage points, and in doing so, increase their fraction of participants from about 40 percent to about 43 percent. Thus, their overall participation level remains about 10 points higher than their "needs," as indicated by eligibility.

The major changes in the profiles of the elderly come about through the income limit reduction for eligibility. In both the eligible and participant population profile, single person and female headed households are better represented than before the 1981 legislation was enacted. Average incomes are also reduced in both populations. Thus, the impact of the 1981 amendments favored the elderly overall. The amendments also are predicted to result in a larger fraction of housing assistance subsidies to poorer elderly households, to those headed by women, and to those made up of single elderly individuals.

TABLE 4-8
SUMMARY OF THE EFFECTS OF 1981 LEGISLATION

Eligible Population	*Nonelderly Headed Households*	*Elderly Headed Households*	*All Households*
All Prior Rules			
Number of Households	7,649	2,860	10,509
50 Percent of Median Rule			
Number of Households	4,190	1,935	6,125
Percent Change	−45.2	−32.2	−41.7
Percent Distribution			
(Pre/Post 1981)	72.9/68.4	27.2/31.6	

Program Participants	*Nonelderly Headed Households*	*Elderly Headed Households*	*All Households*
All Prior Rules			
Number of Households	1,737	1,151	2,888
50 Percent of Median Rule Only			
Number of Households	1,258	899	2,157
Percent Change	−27.6	−21.9	−25.3
Standardized Deductions Only			
Number of Households	1,737	1,151	2,888
Percent Change	(a)	(a)	(a)
30 Percent Tenant Contribution Only			
Number of Households	1,542	1,021	2,565
Percent of Change	−11.2	−11.3	−11.2
All 1981 Rules Combined			
Number of Households	1,143	848	1,991
Percent Change	−34.2	−26.3	−31.1
Percent Distribution			
(Pre/Post 1981)	60.1/57.4	39.8/42.5	

Note: Number of households in thousands.

(a) less than .05 percent

APPENDIX TO CHAPTER FOUR

HUD's Household Size Adjustment for Income Limits

One structural aspect of the income limit merits special attention in the context of assistance for the elderly. The particular way HUD adjusts the income limit for various household sizes leads to some inequities which, in fact, favor certain types of elderly households. Rather than calculating the median family income for households of each size in a particular geographical area, HUD calculates only one figure—that for all families in the area. As table A-1 shows, this figure was then multiplied by .8 prior to the 1981 regulations, and by .5 thereafter for households with four persons. For every other household size, a predetermined percentage is applied, as the table shows. For one person households, for example, their income limit is set at 35 percent of the area median income for all families under the 1981 rules. Their income limit was not calculated as 50 percent of the area median incomes for all households of one person.

Does this household size adjustment make a difference? Here a rough approximation, using national medians, provides a test of which household sizes benefit from the way HUD performs the calculation. Table A-2 shows 50 percent of actual national median income for each household size. In the second column, the HUD formula limits are listed, based on the median income for all families and applying percentages for each household size listed in table A-1. The third column contains a simple ratio of these two numbers.

The greater the ratio, the bigger the advantage of any household size in qualifying for the program under HUD's formula. As the table shows, this ratio is between .85 and 1.15 for household sizes of two or more persons. The one notable outlyer is for one-person households, who are at an advantage, given HUD's household size adjustment procedure. Recall that, for the most part, the household eligibility rules prohibit participation by nonelderly single persons who are not disabled or handicapped. Thus, the advantage to one-person households largely benefits elderly persons living alone.

TABLE A-1
INCOME ELIGIBILITY LIMITS BY HOUSEHOLD SIZE
BEFORE AND AFTER 1981 AMENDMENTS

Household Size	*Percent of Area Median Income All Families* — *Pre-1981 Rule*	*1981 Rule*
1 person	56	35
2 persons	64	40
3 persons	72	45
4 persons	80	50
5 persons	85	54
6 persons	90	58
7 persons	95	62
8+ persons	100	66

SOURCE: Section 8—Housing Assistance Payment Program—Existing Housing. (A HUD Handbook 7420.3 Rev.) Washington, D.C., June 1978. Regulations to implement the 1981 Amendments incorporated adjustment factors previously used for "very-low income" families, i.e., those with incomes less than 50 percent of area median.

TABLE A-2
INCOME ELIGIBILITY LIMITS, USING ACTUAL MEDIANS
FOR EACH HOUSEHOLD SIZE AND HUD FORMULA

Size of Household	*(a) 50 Percent of National Median*	*(b) HUD Formula*	*(c) Ratio (b/a)*
1 person	$2,954	$5,606	1.93
2 persons	6,445	6,403	.99
3 persons	8,177	7,204	.88
4 persons	9,362	8,004	.85
5 persons	9,568	8,644	.90
6 persons	9,628	9,285	.96
7 persons	8,598	9,926	1.15

SOURCE: *Current Population Survey* (Series P-60, No. 116), July 1978. HUD formula is based on a national median income for all households of $16,009.

Chapter 5

COUNTING FOOD STAMPS

In the previous chapter we considered changes in the system of housing assistance enacted into law in 1981. These changes had varying degrees of impact on the size and makeup of the eligible population and are also likely to change the participating population over time. Here we consider a proposed change—counting food stamps as income for purposes of determining eligibilty and for calculating a household's subsidy level.

Currently, food stamps are not counted as income in either eligibility determination or subsidy calculation. Indeed, the entire system of income transfer programs contains a number of cases where exceptions are made for "in-kind" income. These include housing subsidies themselves, food stamps, and medicaid payments.

Several reasons have been put forward for the exclusion of in-kind income from countable income. First, in-kind subsidies do not always permit the same kind of discretion for spending that a household is allowed through other forms of income, such as wages. In addition, some administrative problems are encountered in counting in-kind benefits, especially when such benefits are not received on a regular and steady basis, as in the case of medical care payments.

These arguments, however, no longer hold for the food stamp program because a copayment on the part of the participating household is no longer required. Food stamps are issued solely on the basis of household income, not on the basis of how much the household decides to spend on food stamps. Furthermore, while food stamps are intended to go for food items only, the broad choice permitted for households makes the stamps virtually equivalent to cash.

If this is so, equitable treatment of households would require counting food stamps as income. On other grounds, however, counting food stamps might not be a good idea, particularly since it might result in less targeting of the housing subsidy to those in need. Through analysis of the impact on eligible and participating households, we will be able to test this outcome.

Before looking specifically at what happens when food stamps are counted, one must ask what percentage of eligibles and participants receive food stamps. Assuming that the 1981 legislative amendments are fully implemented, there is a small difference between the elderly and the nonelderly in this regard. Twenty-five percent of the elderly and 28 percent of the nonelderly in the post-1981 population of eligibles receive food stamps. This is the same 1983 eligible population discussed in chapter four. Participants (once the 1981 amendments are implemented) receive food stamps at a slightly higher level than the eligible population; and, again, there is a difference between the elderly and the nonelderly. Thirty-six percent of the elderly and 31 percent of nonelderly program participants receive some food stamps. Does this make a difference in the size and makeup of the eligible and participatng populations?

Impact on Eligibles

Here we assume that the 1981 changes are already in effect and that food stamps are counted as income for 1983 eligibles. Table 5-1 shows the result of this further program change. The top panel of the table recalls the result from the previous chapter when the new income limit of 50 percent of the area median was employed. About 48 percent of elderly headed households and 24 percent of nonelderly headed households in SMSAs were eligible when these rules were put in force.

Counting food stamps reduces the overall eligible population by about 4 percent, with very little difference between elderly headed and nonelderly headed households. The magnitude of this change is quite a bit smaller than the one observed earlier for the reduction in the income limit (around 42 percent). The numbers are also consistent with the figures cited above on food stamp recipiency, because the elderly eligible receive food stamps at a slightly lower rate, and are made ineligible once food stamps are counted at a lower rate.

The effect of counting food stamps on a profile of the eligible elderly population is shown in table 5-2. As the table indicates, these changes are very small, and for no single household characteristic does the percentage change exceed one percent. But as the table also shows, if food stamps are counted the average income of eligible elderly households increases by about $200. The impact of counting food stamps on the types of the eligible elderly appears very small, but a population with higher cash income becomes eligible as a result of this change.

TABLE 5-1
COUNTING FOOD STAMPS AS INCOME: EFFECT ON THE ELIGIBLE POPULATION

	Nonelderly Headed Households	*Elderly Headed Households*	*All Households*
PANEL A			
NOT COUNTING FOOD STAMPS*			
Number of Eligible Households (thousands)	4,109	1,935	6,125
Percent of All Households in Age of Head Category	23.5	47.9	28.5
Percent of All Eligible Households	68.4	31.6	100.0
PANEL B			
COUNTING FOOD STAMPS			
Number of Eligible Households (thousands)	4,034	1,866	5,900
Percent of All Households in Age of Head Category	23.1	46.1	27.4
Percent of All Eligible Households	68.3	31.6	100.0
Percent Change in Eligibility By Counting Food Stamps	−3.7	−3.6	−3.7

SOURCE: Urban Institute TRIM Model.

a. Assumes prior imposition of all legislative changes discussed in chapter 4.

Impact on Participants

As we observed in the previous chapter, the size of the impact of a rule change for the eligible population is not always equivalent to the change in the participating population. Here we again assume that the 1981 amendments are in place. Table 5-3 shows the effect of counting food stamps on the eligibility of 1983 housing program participants. The top panel recalls previous information on the participating population after 1981 changes are made. The elderly constitute about 43 percent of all participants under these conditions.

Counting food stamps reduces the overall participating population by about 7 percent, but there is a three point spread between the elderly (−5 percent) and the nonelderly (−8 percent). As a result of this difference, the elderly raise their percentage of the total participating population very slightly.

TABLE 5-2
EFFECT OF COUNTING FOOD STAMPS ON PROFILE OF THE ELDERLY ELIGIBLE POPULATION

	Percent Distribution	
Household Characteristic	Not Counting Food Stamps	Counting Food Stamps
Race of Head		
White	77.5%	78.1%
Black	16.0	15.9
Hispanic	4.7	4.5
Other	1.7	1.6
Sex of Head		
Male	28.0	27.2
Female	71.9	72.7
Household Size		
1	85.4	86.3
2	12.0	11.3
3–4	2.3	2.0
5+	.3	.2
Household Composition		
Single	85.4	86.3
Couples	11.6	10.9
Others	3.0	2.8
Major Source of Income		
Earnings	3.7	3.6
Social Security	77.9	78.2
AFDC	1.0	1.0
SSI	10.7	10.8
Unemployment Compensation	.2	.3
Pensions	4.2	3.8
No Income	2.1	2.2
Age of Elderly Head		
$> 62 \leq 75$ years	61.5	61.3
75+ years	38.5	38.7
Average Annual Income	\$5,527	\$5,719

SOURCE: Urban Institute TRIM Model.

a. Figures do not always add to 100 because of rounding.

TABLE 5-3
EFFECT OF COUNTING FOOD STAMPS ON ELIGIBILITY OF HOUSING PROGRAMS PARTICIPANTS

	Nonelderly Headed Households	*Elderly Headed Households*	*All Households*
PANEL A			
Housing Program Participants[a]			
Number of Participants (thousands)	1,143	848	1,991
Percent of all Participants	57.4	42.5	100.0
PANEL B			
Housing Program Participants Under Rule of Counting Food Stamps			
Number of Participants	1,049	803	1,852
Percent of all Participants	56.6	43.4	100.0
Percent Change in Eligible Participants	−8.2	−5.3	−7.0

SOURCE: Urban Institute TRIM Model.

a. Assumes prior imposition of all legislative changes discussed in chapter 4.

These results are again consistent with earlier figures showing elderly participants less likely to be receiving food stamps anyway.

The change in the profile for the elderly participants when food stamps are counted are in table 5-4, and the results are very similar to the impact on the elderly eligibles. None of the household characteristics show much change, with the exception of average incomes. The average income of elderly participants is about $200 greater when food stamps are counted as when they are not.

Thus, counting food stamps does not adversely affect the elderly compared to the nonelderly, in either the size of the eligibles or the size of participating households. The change does, however, target resources to higher income households. The next chapter presents estimates of the reduction in housing subsidies that results from counting food stamps as income.

TABLE 5-4
EFFECT OF COUNTING FOOD STAMPS ON THE PROFILE OF ELDERLY HOUSING PROGRAM PARTICIPANTS

Household Characteristic	*Percent Distribution* Not Counting Food Stamps	Counting Food Stamps
Race of Head		
White	72.6	73.6
Black	21.3	20.7
Hispanic	4.7	4.4
Other	1.3	1.2
Sex of Head		
Male	23.0	21.6
Female	77.0	78.4
Household Size		
1	87.9	89.7
2	9.2	7.7
3–4	2.9	2.6
5+	0	.0
Household Composition		
Single	87.9	89.7
Couples	8.8	7.2
Other	3.3	3.1
Major Source of Income		
Earnings	1.9	2.0
Social Security	77.7	78.8
AFDC	1.6	1.3
SSI	14.2	14.3
Pensions	4.0	3.1
No Income	.7	.5
Age of Elderly Head		
$> 62 \leq 75$ years	62.7	63.0
75+ years	37.3	37.0
Average Annual Income	$5,220	$5,434

SOURCE: Urban Institute TRIM Model.

a. Figures do not always add to 100 because of rounding.

Chapter 6

ELDERLY RENTERS AND VOUCHER PROGRAMS

Earlier chapters have detailed the structure of the Section 8 Existing program, whereby the effective demand for housing of a low-income household is augmented so that it can afford to rent an adequate quality dwelling. Housing vouchers, which the Reagan administration proposes, are simply a variation of this same approach.

The voucher idea has been tested extensively in the Experimental Housing Allowance Program (EHAP), which is described more fully below. The principal differences between the Section 8 Existing program and housing vouchers as administered in EHAP appear in table 6-1. The changes generally increase the responsibility placed on participants (as opposed to the administering agency) and give the participant greater incentive for being a careful shopper with the voucher. Under the voucher, the size of the subsidy is calculated in terms of area market rents and is invariant with the rent of the unit chosen by the household. Thus, if the household rents a unit for less than the established market rent for its area, it can keep the extra subsidy and spend it on other things. In this sense, the household is rewarded for finding a unit that meets the standard and still rents for less than the established market rent. On the other hand, if the household chooses to rent for more than the established market rent, it must pay the difference itself, since the upper bound of the subsidy is the area market rent.

Thus, how "market rents" are computed is a critical issue, and one that will be discussed in detail below. The Reagan administration's FY 1983 budget proposal is for a voucher program very similar in *structure* to the one tested in EHAP as the primary vehicle for assisting low-income households to live in adequate housing. The program, labeled the "Modified Section 8 Certificate Program," alters the current Section 8 program to bring it in line

TABLE 6-1
PRINCIPAL DIFFERENCES BETWEEN HOUSING VOUCHERS AND SECTION 8 EXISTING HOUSING PROGRAM

	Section 8 Existing Housing	*Housing Vouchers*[a]
Nature of Payment	Payment made to landlord on behalf of assisted household. Requires contract between administering agency and landlord.	Payment made directly to assisted household. No contract between agency and landlord required.
Rent/Subsidy Limit	Maximum allowable rent levels limit households' housing choices and size of subsidy.	No maximum rents apply. Subsidy cap limits federal expenditure but households may choose any physically standard units and pay the difference themselves.
Size of Subsidy	Subsidy equals difference between rent on participant unit and fixed percent of tenant income. Subsidy varies with household income and rent on participant unit.	Subsidy equals difference between area market rents and fixed percent of tenant income. Subsidy varies only with household income.

a. The voucher alternative described here is the primary program design used in the Experimental Housing Allowance Program.

with the voucher program tested in EHAP. However, while the structure is similar, the administration has chosen key *parameters* that determine the size of the subsidy a household would receive, which differ from any tested in EHAP. In particular, the proposal changes the manner in which the area market rent is calculated, thereby lowering subsidy size, as we shall see.

The tasks of this chapter are (1) to discuss the process by which a family—particularly the elderly—come to receive housing assistance under a voucher program, using evidence from EHAP; and (2) to evaluate how the elderly are likely to fare under the administration's specific proposal for a voucher program, including the manner by which subsidy size is calculated.

Becoming a Voucher Recipient

To become a recipient in a housing voucher program the applicant must get enrolled and then find a dwelling that can be certified as meeting the program's requirements. To become enrolled, a family must learn of the program, decide that the program is of sufficient benefit to it to apply, and provide the administering agency with the necessary documentation about its income so that the family's eligibility for the program can be determined. The agency takes the application, determines eligibility, and, if the household is eligible, issues it a certificate which usually gives the family a specified amount of time to find a unit of acceptable quality.[1]

Once enrolled, the family must find a dwelling that meets the program's standards. The family can nominate the unit it is living in for inspection by the agency staff, or any other unit. If the family lives in a unit that meets the standards, it can begin receiving payments. If not, it must induce the landlord to make the necessary repairs, make the repairs themselves, move to a unit that does qualify, or (eventually) drop out of the program.

Table 6-2 illustrates the experience of households working their way through the two steps required to become a recipient, using data from the "Supply Experiment" element of EHAP.[2] The table is organized to give three figures for each household group specified: (1) enrollment rates, that is, the percentage of eligible households who actually fill out the application forms and are told that if they find program-acceptable housing they will receive payments; (2) the rate at which enrollees become recipients, that is, the rate at which they find and lease acceptable housing; and (3) the rate at which eligible households become recipients, that is, the product of (2) and (1). It is the last set of rates that answers the question usually posed about program participation; these are found in the last column of the table.

Note that these rates vary sharply among the household types distinguished in the table. Ultimately, about one elderly household in three receives payments, whereas among the nonelderly the rate is about two in five. These low recipiency rates for the elderly resulted even after extensive outreach efforts in both sites. Note too, that the recipiency rates of specific groups of the elderly and nonelderly overlap, so broad generalizations about the elderly rates would be inaccurate.

The table also shows that elderly couples receive payments at lower rates than elderly single persons. It is anticipated that participation is influenced by the size of the subsidy, and, because single persons have lower incomes than couples, a higher participation rate is expected for them.

Unfortunately, reliable data on black households are limited. In South Bend, nonelderly blacks become recipients at rates at least as high as their

TABLE 6-2
PARTICIPATION RATES BY RENTERS IN AN ENTITLEMENT VOUCHER PROGRAM, END OF SECOND YEAR[a]
(Percent)

	Eligible Households Enrolled[b]	*Enrollees Becoming Recipients*	*Eligibles Becoming Recipients*
South Bend, Indiana			
White households			
Nonelderly			
Young couple, young children	32	63	20
Single head with children	63	75	47
Other	48	73	35
Elderly			
Elderly couple	20	80	16
Elderly single person	38	82	31
Minority households			
Nonelderly			
Young couple, young children	37	61	23
Single head with children	c	67	c
Other	68	67	45
Elderly			
Elderly couple	c	58	c
Elderly single person	33	73	24
Green Bay, Wisconsin			
All households			
Nonelderly			
Young couple, young children	40	73	29
Single head with children	69	84	54
Other	70	81	57
Elderly			
Elderly couple	30	82	25
Elderly single person	46	89	41

SOURCE: Struyk-Soldo (1981), table 7-10.

a. Includes only those enrolling at least six months before the end of year 2, so as to exclude most of those still repairing their dwellings or looking for alternatives.

b. The observation dates for eligibility and enrollment differ by about two years, during which the number of eligibles may have changed. About one-third of all enrollees terminated enrollment before the end of year; they are not counted in the enrollment rate.

c. Based on less than ten survey records, to establish the eligible population; or too few enrollees for reliable estimate.

white counterparts. For elderly single persons, though, blacks achieve recipiency status at a lower rate than similar white households (31 versus 24 percent). Based on a single city, these figures must be considered cautiously.

The other columns in the table reveal systematic differences between the elderly and nonelderly in how these ultimate recipiency rates are reached. Among renters in South Bend, the elderly enroll at lower rates than the nonelderly; but they move from enrollment to recipiency status at significantly higher rates than the nonelderly. In Green Bay the picture is similar, but the rates for some nonelderly and elderly household types overlap. In South Bend, black renters enroll at higher rates than whites when similar household types are observed, but blacks, both among the elderly and nonelderly, consistently move from enrollment to recipiency status at lower rates.

Before leaving this introduction to participation, an additional point is essential. In the experiments, income eligibility corrsponded roughly with the 80 percent of local area median income. (Actually, it was established as four times the fair market rent.) As noted, the income eligibility limit for the Section 8 program was lowered to 50 percent of area median income by 1981 legislation. This change significantly increases participation rates, since lower income households participate at higher rates than their somewhat higher income counterparts. Table 6-3 documents this point in a tabulation based on unpublished data from the fourth year of the Supply Experiment.

TABLE 6-3
PERCENTAGE OF ELIGIBLE RENTER HOUSEHOLDS BECOMING HOUSING ALLOWANCE RECIPIENTS IN THE SUPPLY EXPERIMENT UNDER ALTERNATIVE ELIGIBILITY RULES

	Eligibility Definition	
	50 percent of area median income	*80 percent of area median income*
South Bend		
Elderly couples	31	20
Elderly individuals	51	44
All households	53	37
Green Bay		
Elderly couples	40	30
Elderly Individuals	78	65
All households	60	43

The broad patterns reviewed above generally continue to hold; but participation rates are sharply higher—overall about one-third higher. Unfortunately, very little separate analysis has been conducted to date of the experience of lower income households in the experiments. For this reason, the figures presented below are for the full experimental population. However, one should be aware of the possibility of changes in the facts presented when only the lower income population is studied.

To allow a better understanding of the factors determining the likelihood of enrollment and qualifying for payments by finding a unit meeting program standards, the next section will amplify on what has been learned from the Supply Experiment segment of EHAP. The section thereafter uses data from the "Demand Experiment" to analyze the likely impact of the reductions in the benefits implicit in the Reagan administration's proposal. First, however, the rationale for our choice of data bases for these analyses requires an overall understanding of the EHAP experiments as a whole.

The experiment was complicated in structure because of the many questions to be answered. Three field operations were established, each focusing on a different set of questions:

- The *Demand Experiment* involved about 1,800 households in Phoenix and another 1,800 in Pittsburgh. Its goal was to reveal the way households would react to housing vouchers in terms of participation, household mobility, and housing consumption. It also sought to learn how households' reactions and program outcomes varied under alternative forms of voucher programs involving different payment formulas, varying generosity of benefits, and minimum housing consumption requirements.
- The *Supply Experiment* involved over 25,000 households in Green Bay, Wisconsin, and South Bend, Indiana. The purpose of the Supply Experiment was to raise the level of demand for housing services within a housing market up to the level likely to be attained if a nationwide housing voucher program were instituted. It did this by operating an open enrollment program in each site for a decade, and monitoring the outcomes for half that period. This permitted observation of the reactions of suppliers of housing services in terms of increase in the quantity, quality, and price of housing services. It also was designed to probe community and institutional reactions (including those of real estate brokers and mortgage lenders) to a full-scale allowance program.
- The *Administrative Agency Experiment* (*AAE*) involved between 400 and 900 households at each of eight sites scattered widely across the

United States. This experiment emphasized the behavior of administering agencies in the "real world" of actual program operations. Thus, while the voucher programs in the other two experiments were operated by special agencies created by the research organizations, in the AAE they were administered by existing agencies, state or local.

Enrolling in a Voucher Program

This section draws on analysis of the experience in the Supply Experiment to explore the enrollment process and to determine if the elderly have systematically different outcomes compared to the nonelderly, as suggested by the data presented earlier.[3] This experiment was operated in Green Bay and South Bend and was open to both homeowners and renters. Many of the findings reported here are for the two groups together; only where separate findings by tenure are important are they mentioned.

The Supply Experiment offers the best opportunity to observe the behavior of households that are exposed to the possibility of participating in this type of program because of the open enrollment character of the programs. All other experience with housing vouchers and the Section 8 Existing program are in situations in which the number of households that can be assisted is less than the number of eligible households who would want to participate if they could. Profiles of participants in these "constrained" programs are sensitive to how the administering agencies advertise the availability of assistance, and possibly to the priorities that agencies set for serving different types of households. The Supply Experiment is essentially free from the biases introduced by these constraints.

Learning about the Program. The first thing to note is that it was very easy for would-be participants to learn about the program. The opening of the program in each site was accompanied by substantial media coverage and both programs conducted very extensive efforts to advertise the program's existence.[4] As the figures in table 6-4 show, at the end of the third year of program operations in each site, the majority of households knew about the

TABLE 6-4

PERCENTAGE OF HOUSEHOLDS KNOWLEDGEABLE ABOUT THE VOUCHER PROGRAM

Age of Head	*Green Bay*	*South Bend*
Under 62	87	86
62 or over	77	85

SOURCE: Wendt (1981).

program.[5] In Green Bay, for some reason, the elderly had somewhat lower knowledge rates than the nonelderly.

Multivariate analysis of whether a household knew about the program uncovers information not found in these simple percentages. Specifically, knowledge rates were related to several types of phenomena:

- *Need for assistance,* as measured by the household's income and housing expenses
- *Life cycle stage,* in which nonelderly parents, the elderly, and others were distinguished
- *Principal source of information,* in which newspapers, television, radio, word of mouth, and public-aid agencies were distinguished
- *Tenure,* that is, homeowners vs. renters

Analysis of these factors showed households less likely to have knowledge were renters, those with higher incomes, and those with low housing expenses. Those more likely to benefit from the program knew about it. Households who relied on the newspaper or a public-aid agency for this type of information were more likely to have knowledge than those relying on other information sources. By far the largest single difference was in the life-cycle variable: after controlling for need, information sources, and tenure, the elderly were about 13 percent less likely to have knowledge than nonelderly families. This is much larger than the simple differences between the two groups reported earlier, and it points to a serious problem for the elderly.

Taking the Next Step. Given that households know about the program, what determines which ones go on to enroll in the program? Four different factors, some of them closely related, have been hypothesized as important: the benefits from participating, the cost of participating, the extent of housing need, and the willingness to accept public assistance. For his analysis of the determinants, Wendt (1981) measured these factors as follows. Benefits were measured as (a) the grant that a household would receive if it qualified for payments, and (b) the number of months the household would be expected to receive payments, based on the experience of similar households.

The costs of participation were captured by determining whether the household had moved recently (implying less effort for another move if one was necessary) and the quality of housing currently occupied (as measured by expenditures), since higher-cost units were more likely to pass inspection without repairs or with only minimal repairs. The cost of participation is also related to the age of the head of household; inertia, especially unwillingness to become involved in a process that requires the person to provide economic information and have a stranger (the dwelling inspector) in one's home is very likely to be greater among the elderly than for younger households.[6]

The cost of participation might be perceived as greater by homeowners than by renters. Homeowners would have to bear the cost of repairs to their homes. If the required repairs were prohibitively expensive, they would face the high transaction costs associated with shifting dwellings.

Aspects of need apart from those already discussed are household size, the extent of crowding, and the amount of nonproperty assets. As to the willingness to accept aid, the data set includes each eligible's response to the question: "Should the national government help low- and moderate-income people get housing at low cost?" Those responding negatively to the question were classified as unwilling to accept help.

The results of the multivariate analysis, summarized in table 6-5, are in many ways parallel to those for the analysis of knowledge acquisition. The center column of the table shows the values of the independent variables compared in computing the difference in the probability given in the final column. Where numeric values appear in the center column they are the interquartile values of the variable.

The size of the benefits under the program are highly significant and numerically large determinants of enrollment. Poor households, especially those expecting to be poor for an extended period, are prime candidates to enroll. The costs of participation as reported in housing costs are generally not significant. This is consistent with other studies which show that costs of participation become important only after enrollment.[7] On the other hand, the elderly enroll at a rate 11 percent less than nonelderly families, after controlling for other factors.

Homeowners are 6 percent less likely to enroll than renters, and households with as little as $1,000 for nonproperty assets are about 10 percent less likely to enroll than those with no such assets. Finally, those households which expressed a negative attitude toward national government assistance for housing back up their statement: they enrolled 13 percent less often than otherwise similar households with a positive attitude.

Enrollment: Summary and Implications. These results can be put in perspective by considering the combined effect of lower knowledge acquisition on elderly enrollment and of lower enrollment rates given knowledge. If we had a pool of nonelderly families and individuals who were similar in all respects except age to a group of elderly-headed families and individuals, then for each 100 nonelderly households who enrolled in this type of voucher program only 77 elderly would have enrolled.

Of course, the nonelderly and elderly differ from each other in many ways that affect enrollment. However, the findings presented here suggest that reliance on vouchers may put the elderly at a disadvantage in competing with other households for housing assistance. Under a closed enrollment

TABLE 6-5
EFFECT OF FACTORS, BY VARIABLE, ON THE DECISION TO APPLY FOR ASSISTANCE IN A HOUSING VOUCHER PROGRAM

Variables	*Values Compared*[a]	Difference in Probability (%)
Benefits		
Amount of payment	$40 vs. $102	7[b]
Duration of eligibility	.92 vs. 12.32 months	16[b]
Costs		
Housing quality:		
Owners	$26 vs. $48	−2
Mobile renters	$34 vs. $50	−3
Nonmobile renters	$26 vs. $48	7[b]
Recently moved	No vs. yes	3[b]
Tenure	Renters vs. owners	−6[c]
Life-cycle stage	Parents vs. elderly	−11[d]
Sense of Need		
Nonproperty assets	0 vs. $944	−10[c]
Household size	1 vs. 3 persons	−3
Crowding:		
Owners	1 vs. .25 per room	23[d]
Renters	1 vs. .25 per room	2
Willingness to Accept Help		
Attitude toward aid	For vs. against	−13[b]

SOURCE: Wendt (1981), table 12.

a. The values compared are for households at the 25th and 75th percentile of the distribution of each characteristic within the total sample of eligible households, when all other values are held at their mean.
b. Significant at .01 level.
c. Significant at .05 level.
d. Significant at .10 level.

program, such as the administration is proposing, there is far less effort to inform households of the availability of assistance since agencies are reluctant to build up expectations in the community when few households can be served. The elderly may enroll at even lower rates than those presented above and thereby be further underrepresented among recipients.

Moving From Enrollment to Recipiency in the Administration's Voucher Program

We have seen that, once enrolled, the elderly were generally successful in becoming recipients in the voucher program operated as part of EHAP's Supply Experiment. The question addressed now is how the combination of actions taken by the Congress in 1981 and proposed by the administration as part of the FY 1983 budget would affect these outcomes. Three actions in particular are germane: congressional action which raises the participant's contribution to housing from 25 to 30 percent of adjusted income; the administration's proposal to count the subsidy value of food stamps as income in computing the participant's contribution; and the reduction in the "Fair Market Rent."

With the exception of the change in Fair Market Rents (FMR), each of the other actions or proposals has been treated in some detail in earlier chapters. Here, it is important to clarify the proposed manner for computing the FMR, because it represents the most direct way in which the subsidy per individual household is to be reduced, when compared to the current Section 8 Existing program.

An important aspect of FMR computations is that Congress does not itself establish the FMR schedule, nor does it specify in a precise way how it should be done. The 1974 legislation establishing the Section 8 program charged the secretary of HUD with determining "fair market rents" for dwellings appropriate for assisted families. In response to this mandate, HUD has set FMRs for the Section 8 Existing program for each Standard Metropolitan Statistical Area (SMSA) and for each nonmetropolitan county. Starting with FMRs effective in 1979, HUD has used the metropolitan Annual Housing Survey (AHS) to provide the basic data. Median rent for *recently occupied* (i.e., within the last year) two-bedroom units without defects were identified from each SMSA survey and updated by the Consumer Price Index to the year in which the FMR was to be estimated. Some FMRs were raised further in response to public comments. The resultant rent became the two-bedroom Fair Market Rent for each area. FMRs for bedroom sizes other than two were set using a 15 percent differential per bedroom; so the FMR for a three-bedroom unit is 115 percent of that for the two bedroom. FMRs for places other than the SMSAs surveyed were derived from the national AHS, discussed in chapter 2 of this study, and from 1970 census data.

The administration proposal alters this process for determining FMRs in two important ways, both of which would result in lower subsidy levels. First, rather than the *median* of the distribution of rents, the proposal calls for setting FMRs at the *40th percentile* of the distribution. Second, instead of computing the figure from the rents for recent movers (which is the rent faced by the household who relocates to meet program standards), the plan is to compute it from all rental units. Regarding the final change, the differences between the two distributions of rents arises because of discounts which landlords typically give long-term tenants in exchange for their being good tenants. Hence, the change proposed is more like going from the 50th to the 35th percentile of the recent movers' rent distribution than from the 50th to the 40th percentile of the same distribution.

For this analysis we use data from the Demand Experiment of EHAP. To provide the necessary foundation, this experiment is briefly discussed below. Following this, the procedures used in making the estimates are outlined and the results of the reestimation of the participation models are presented. Then the implications of the Reagan proposals for the elderly are described.

The Demand Experiment. The purpose of the Housing Allowance Demand Experiment (HADE) was to study the responses of households to the offer to participate in different types of voucher programs. The responses studied included the extent of participation in such programs, changes in housing consumption resulting from participation in a voucher program, and the related effect on households' residential mobility. Two generic types of payment formulae were analyzed in HADE: a housing gap (the type used in the Section 8 program and in the Supply Experiment) and a percentage of rent plan (in which the participant's subsidy is computed simply as a specified share of the rent of the unit occupied by the participant). Because the administration's proposals all involve a housing gap formula, the percentage of rent plan is not discussed here.[8]

As its name implies, a housing gap formula calculates the housing allowance payments to which a household is entitled as the difference between what the household is presumed able to pay for shelter and the presumed cost of adequate housing in that household's community. The formula is

$$P = FMR - bY$$

where

P = maximum potential voucher payment

FMR = the estimated cost of acceptable quality housing for a household of a certain size and composition (the FMR was called C* in HADE)

b = fraction of the household's income the household is expected to contribute toward its housing costs

Y = the household's program-defined income.

P is the maximum potential payment because households were never reimbursed for more than their total actual expenditures for rent (plus utilities, if paid separately); hence, a household's payment might be less than the payment specified by this formula. In the Demand Experiment, twelve of the nineteen treatments tested represented various forms of housing gap payments. The variation among them involved alternative levels of benefits and alternative housing consumption requirements.

One way the level of benefits was varied was through use of alternative values for the FMR, the estimated cost of acceptable quality housing for a household. At each of the Demand Experiment sites, a panel of local housing experts was convened to estimate the rental cost of standard quality housing units appropriate for households of different sizes.[9] Once the FMR was established, the various housing gap treatment cells offered allowances of different degrees of generosity by varying the proportion of FMR used in calculating households' payments with the formula. As figure 6-1 indicates, the three values of the FMR used for the various housing gap treatment cells were 80 percent of FMR, 100 percent of FMR, and 120 percent of FMR.

The second variable manipulated to vary the generosity of allowance benefits was b, the proportion of a household's income the household was expected to contribute toward its rental expenses. As the left-hand column in the figure indicates, this variable was also set at three different levels: 15 percent of income, 25 percent of income, and 35 percent of income; the lower this proportion, the higher the monthly allowance payment which a household would receive. The monthly payment an individual household would receive was influenced by the level of the FMR and b assigned to the treatment cell in which the household found itself and by the income level of that individual household.

Eleven of the twelve housing gap treatment cells offered allowance payments to households only as long as the household occupied a unit meeting some sort of minimum housing consumption requirement. One set of these requirements, utilized in those treatment cells marked one through five in the figure, required that the housing unit pass specific agency-dictated minimum physical quality standards and occupancy standards. The standards addressed such topics as the allowable number of occupants per room, the presence of adequate light, heat, plumbing, and ventilation, and the sound condition of walls, roofs, and floors. Conformity with these standards was monitored by inspections of the housing unit made at the initial enrollment in the program, at one-year intervals thereafter, and at any time the household moved.

In contrast to these five "minimum standards" housing gap treatment groups, six "minimum rent" housing gap treatment groups used a more indirect method of insuring minimum levels of housing consumption. House-

FIGURE 6-1
TREATMENT CELLS AND SAMPLE SIZES IN THE DEMAND EXPERIMENT FOR HOUSING GAP TREATMENTS (P = FMR − bY)

		Housing Requirements			
b value	*FMR Level*	*Minimum Standards*	*Minimum Rent Low = 0.7FMR*	*Minimum Rent High = 0.9FMR*	*Unconstrained*
b = 15% of income	100% of FMR	CELL 1 81 households			
	120% of FMR	CELL 2 63 households	CELL 6 58 households	CELL 9 60 households	
b = 25% of income	100% of FMR	CELL 3 77 households	CELL 7 89 households	CELL 10 88 households	CELL 12 103 households
	80% of FMR	CELL 4 82 households	CELL 8 79 households	CELL 11 78 households	
b = 35% of income	100% of FMR	CELL 5 75 households			

NOTE: Sample sizes are for participants active at two years, with Pittsburgh and Phoenix households combined.

holds receiving payments in these treatment groups were required to maintain at least a specified level of rental expenditures, under the assumption that housing units commanding certain levels of rent would automatically provide housing of certain levels of quality. As figure 6-1 indicates, three of these treatment groups, called "high minimum rent" treatments, required households to spend at least 90 per cent of FMR monthly, while the remaining three treatment groups, called "low minimum rent," required households to spend at least 70 percent of FMR.

The final housing gap treatment cell, number 12 in the figure, was designated the "unconstrained" treatment group. Households in this group were free to choose whatever housing they wished to occupy, constrained by neither minimum rent requirements nor minimum standards of housing quality. The behavior of this group thus established a baseline against which the effects of the housing consumption requirements could be measured.

It is important to understand how "eligible" households were defined in HADE to appreciate our analysis strategy. Unlike the Supply Experiment, the program was not open to all households who fulfilled the basic income and other eligibility criteria.[10] Only a set of households randomly selected were offered a chance to participate. No general publicity about the allowance program was undertaken; instead, an interviewer went to the homes of the selected households and informed them that they had been chosen for participation in a housing survey. The interviewer then administered a "screening interview" to determine if the household was eligible for the program in terms of the criteria described. Households' responses to these initial questions were reviewed at the experiment's site office, and each household that appeared to be program-eligible was randomly assigned to one of nineteen treatment cells within the experiment.[11] These households were then reinterviewed and subsequently sent letters explaining the experiment and the benefits which the allowance program would offer them. The letters invited them to attend individual interviews at the site office for enrollment.

When a member of a household appeared for his enrollment interview, site staff asked further questions to insure that the household was actually eligible for allowance benefits. The staff also described the rules of the program (appropriate to the treatment cell to which the household had been assigned) and provided an estimate of the monthly benefits the household would receive if it chose to participate.

If the household decided to enroll in the voucher program, the site office completed the enrollment process. A housing inspection was performed on the unit occupied by the household at the time of application, and a final calculation of benefits was made. For those under the minimum standards rules, the household began receiving payments if the unit passed inspection.

Otherwise, payments did not begin until the family resided in a qualifying unit.

Because of this unique way in which would-be participants' interest in the program was solicited, the results of the enrollment process in HADE are of comparatively little interest. Once enrolled, however, would-be participants had to negotiate the same steps to receive payments as applicants in the Section 8 program or the Supply Experiment, and it is those steps upon which we focus.

Reanalysis of HADE Data. Prior analysis undertaken within the Demand Experiment examined the probability of households moving from enrollment to payment recipient irrespective of the age of the head of household. Here we have reanalyzed HADE data, dividing enrollee households into those with elderly heads and those with nonelderly heads.

The most convenient starting point is to contrast the transition experience of the elderly and nonelderly. The figures reported in table 6-6 are based on households that remained "active" in the experiment over the two-year period during which monitoring surveys were conducted. Being active required at minimum that the household complete various reports and interviews (for which it was paid). We chose this group as the base population of the study to permit the maximum amount of time for enrollees to become participants. It seems especially appropriate to take this longer view for the elderly, since their incomes tend to be quite stable and thus they would be persistent if eligible for assistance. Additionally, one can conceive of an elderly renter qualifying at the time he or she relocates. Using the active-at-two-year population thus will tend to give an optimistic view of the likelihood of participation.

The figures in the table must, however, be interpreted in light of a strongly countervailing factor for the minimum standards program. That is, the physical standards applied in the Demand Experiment were significantly more stringent than those applied in the Supply Experiment and the Section 8 Existing program. This factor in part accounts for the difference in the rate at which enrollees become recipients in the Demand Experiment versus the Supply Experiment; for nonelderly welfare recipients who rented, for example, the rate was 52 percent in the Demand Experiment versus 70 percent in the Supply Experiment.[12]

Turning now to the figures actually in the table, it is seen that the elderly moved from enrollment to participation at lower rates than their nonelderly counterparts for all three of the housing gap programs. The Minimum Standards program is of particular interest. Among the elderly, 48 percent of those who eventually become participants lived in units that met requirements at

TABLE 6-6
PARTICIPATION RATES AT TWO YEARS IN THE HOUSING GAP ALLOWANCE PROGRAMS IN THE DEMAND EXPERIMENT BY TYPE OF PROGRAM AND AGE OF HOUSEHOLD HEAD
(Percentages)

	Type of Program					
	Minimum Standard		*Minimum Rent-Low*		*Minimum Rent-High*	
	Nonelderly	*Elderly*[a]	*Nonelderly*	*Elderly*[a]	*Nonelderly*	*Elderly*[a]
Percentage of all enrollees participating at 2 years	54	48	86	67	57	44
Percentage of all enrollees who met requirements at enrollment	18	24	54	47	24	24
Percentage of enrollees who did not meet requirements at enrollment who eventually met requirements	46	33	71	37	45	26
Percentage of all participants at 2 years who met requirements at enrollment	30	48	62	71	40	55
(Number of enrollees active at 2 years)	(250)	(92)	(144)	(57)	(156)	(46)

SOURCE: Analysis of data from the Housing Allowance Demand Experiment.

a. An elderly household head is a person 62 years of age or older.

enrollment, a figure substantially higher than the 30 percent for the nonelderly. The other 70 percent of the nonelderly ultimately receiving payments had to upgrade their units or relocate to units that passed the inspection. Eventually, 48 percent of all elderly enrollees received subsidy payments, but only one-third of the elderly who did not meet requirements at enrollment had received payments by the end of two years.

In summary, elderly enrollees became payment recipients at lower rates than the nonelderly, even though they more often lived in units that met requirements at enrollment. The elderly who failed requirements at the outset were quite unlikely to eventually receive payments.

In structuring the formal analysis of the probability of participation, given that a household enrolled in the program, we have followed the lead of Kennedy and MacMillan (1980) in their original analysis for all households. The first point to note is that the population of those who become participants is divided into two groups, those who meet program standards at enrollment, and thus are eligible to begin receiving payments at that time, and those who did not meet the program's requirements at enrollment but who eventually did so. The analysis here is of those households who did *not* meet requirements at enrollment. This constitutes about 69 percent of all elderly headed households who enrolled in the three housing gap programs.

The basic idea is that the household will take whatever action necessary to meet the program's requirements if the housing benefits significantly exceed the cost of meeting the requirements. The value of the benefits are the subsidy payment itself, some of which might be spent on other goods if the subsidy is greater than costs incurred, and the value to the household of the improved housing it obtained under the program. Against these benefits are several costs: the household will probably have to pay a higher rent (for a better unit) than it would have otherwise, and it may incur various out-of-pocket costs such as those associated with looking for a new unit and moving to it.

Since the values of many of the variables just listed are not known with certainty, it is necessary to shift to a stochastic formulation of the problem. In particular, the model can be expressed as follows using variables that can be observed:

$$N = a_0 + a_1R_R + a_2R_O + a_3P_M + a_4S_O + d \qquad (6.1)$$

where

N = the net value to the household of participating

R_R = the required expenditure level (for Minimum Rent households) or the estimated cost of standard housing (for Minimum Standards households)

R_O = the household's housing expenditures at enrollment

P_M = the estimated probability that a household would normally move in the absence of the allowance offer
S_O = the allowance payment at enrollment
d = a stochastic term

The expected sign of a_1 is negative, i.e., the higher the rent required to participate, the lower the net value of participating because the household will have to devote an increasing share of its available resources (including the subsidy) to housing. By similar logic, the sign of a_2 should be positive, i.e., the higher the household's "normal" housing preference and final consumption, the more likely it will highly value incremental housing services close to their cost of production.[13]

Normal housing expenditures, or more broadly, the normal probability of meeting any housing requirements, should also depend on the likelihood that the household would move. We know that major changes in housing consumption, such as significantly upgrading the quality of the unit inhabited often can be accomplished only by shifting dwelling units. All of the households being considered in the present analysis failed to meet the program's requirements at enrollment. It follows that those families who in any event would be moving over the next months would be more apt to become participants, since the cost of meeting requirements is low when one is already changing dwellings. Hence, the sign of a_3 is expected to be positive. Finally, we also expect the sign of a_4 to be positive: the larger the subsidy, the greater its value to the households.

The equation written above can be rewritten into the specification that will actually be estimated as follows:

$$\pi E = a_O + a_1(R_R - R_O) + a_2P_M + a_3S_1 + a_4S_2 + a_5Z \qquad (6.2)$$

where

πE = the probability that a household participated
R_R = the required expenditure level (for Minimum Rent households) or the estimated cost of standard housing (for Minimum Standards households)
R_O = the household's housing expenditures at enrollment
P_M = the estimated probability that a household would normally move in the absence of the allowance offer
S_1 = the payment level at enrollment (computed as the payment the household would have received as a household of size four with the sample mean income)
S_2 = the residual payment (the difference between the actual payment offered at enrollment and S_1), and
Z = household characteristics.

This formulation differs from the prior formulation in three aspects. First, it expresses the probability of participation rather than the net value to the household of participating, it being assumed that the two are very highly correlated. Second, it combines the required housing expenditures (R_R) and normal expenditures (R_O) into a single variable, which can be conveniently thought of as indicating the incremental expenditure—and house size of housing adjustment, including possibly relocating—necessary to become a participant.

Finally, the new formulation splits the subsidy payment into two components. The reasoning is based on the fact that a household's payment depends on the size of the household (because this determines the unit size for the applicable FMR) and the household's income. Both of these factors may change over time. Still, the would-be participant has a general idea of the payment offer. The variable S_1 is to capture the "constant" portion of the payment as it is defined in the mind of the enrollee. S_2, then, accounts for the difference between this "constant" portion and the payment level actually applicable to the household at a particular point in time.

The plan is to estimate equation (6.2) using enrollees who have been offered subsidy payments under the minimum standards and minimum rent programs. The coefficients of the equation are not expected to be the same for minimum rent and minimum standards requirements, both because the relationship between the normal probability of meeting requirements and rent is more tenuous for minimum standards and because the payment amount needed to induce a household to meet minimum standards should be larger than that required under minimum rent for a given change in expenditures. This is based on the fact that physical standards represent a more stringent form of earmarking than the minimum rent requirement. On the other hand, differences in participation under the two minimum rent plans (minimum rent low and minimum rent high) should be captured by changes in the value of R_R. Thus coefficients for these two groups are expected to be similar. Additionally, with the exception of payment variables, the coefficients for variables in Equation (6.2) may reflect both the effects on the normal probability that a household will have met requirements and the further effects on its willingness to participate under a given payment offer.

The estimated models are presented in table 6-7.[14] For comparison, estimates for nonelderly households are included in the table. Of particular interest in this context are the results for the independent variable listed under the heading "Minimum standards households" in the left-hand margin. A glance at the coefficients and associated t-statistics for these variables in the model estimated for elderly households shows that none of the variables are statistically significant. This means that even after two years whether or not

TABLE 6-7
REGRESSION ESTIMATES OF THE PROBABILITY OF PARTICIPATING AT THE END OF TWO YEARS FOR HOUSING GAP HOUSEHOLDS THAT DID NOT MEET REQUIREMENTS AT ENROLLMENT

	Elderly Households		*Nonelderly Households*	
	Coefficient	*t-statistics*	*Coefficient*	*t-statistics*
Constant	.182		.122	
Household in Phoenix (1 = yes)	.364[a]	3.31	.030	.39
Minimum standards households				
Distance ($R_R - R_O$)	−.002	1.04	−.004[a]	3.27
Probability of moving (P_M)	.178	.61	.410[a]	2.91
Payment level (S_1)	.001	.70	.004[a]	4.40
Residual (S_2)	−.006	1.45	.001	.86
Minimum rent households				
Constant	.078	.42	.230	1.77
Distance ($R_R - R_O$)	−.012[a]	4.13	−.007[a]	5.67
Probability of moving (P_M)	.267	.65	.305[a]	2.06
Payment level (S_1)	.003	.89	.002[a]	2.20
Residual Payment (S_2)	.007[a]	2.50	.003[a]	3.00
Summary Statistics				
Adjusted R^2	.19		.19	
F	3.60		8.76	
N-K-1	99		311	
Standard error	.43		.45	
Mean value of dependent variable	.35		.48	

SOURCE: Analysis of HADE data.

a. Significant at the .05 level or greater.

an elderly headed household that did not meet requirements at enrollment eventually became a program participant was essentially random. That is, participation did not depend systematically on the size of the offer, the initial housing situation, or the likelihood that the household would relocate over the period.

It is important to view these findings against those for the nonelderly. Nonelderly households in the minimum standards group responded systematically to payment levels and other factors in the ways that had been hypothesized earlier. One way to interpret the differences between the elderly and nonelderly is to say that participation by the elderly failing to meet requirements at enrollment depends critically on factors not included in the estimated statistical model—such things as assistance in dealing with landlords to get necessary repairs or improvements made or help in finding a unit in their neighborhood that would pass the program standards, plus possibly further help with actually relocating. On balance, the findings for the elderly are mildly surprising, but they are well within the outcomes one might expect given the difficulties that the elderly have traditionally exhibited in making housing adjustments.

The Reagan Voucher Proposals and the Elderly. The changes from the Section 8 Existing program (as constituted in 1980) proposed by the Reagan administration are large by any standard. The figures in table 6-8 summarize the impact of these changes on the size of the subsidy received by program participants. A further word of explanation about these calculations is in order. The population was the 1983 "aged" participants in housing assistance programs, discussed in chapter 4. An applicable Section 8 Existing payment was computed for each household, then new payments were computed for each of several proposed program changes and, then all changes combined. Any household that no longer received a positive payment for the all-changes-combined calculations were dropped from the population of households being analyzed. Thus the figures in the table are for those households who would still be receiving a positive subsidy payment under the most restricted set of benefit rules.

The figures in the table show that for elderly individuals, benefits decline by 15 percent because of the change enacted in 1981 that increased the participant's contribution to rent from 25 to 30 percent of income. The proposed lowering of the FMRs by itself (i.e., ignoring other changes) would reduce benefits to the same group on average by 25 percent. By contrast, counting the subsidy value of food stamps drops benefits by only 5 percent. This is the average effect. As noted elsewhere, the reductions in benefits are greater for the poorest households. Estimates that we have done for Chicago suggest about a 20 percent reduction for those receiving food stamps, with food stamp recipients having incomes below the 30 percent of the area median income.

Considering the combined effects of the change enacted in 1981 and those proposed in the FY 1983 budget, the typical elderly individual participating before and after the changes would have benefits slashed by 44 percent. For elderly couples the figure is 51 percent.

Such reductions in benefits can have three kinds of effects: (1) they cause some households to become ineligible, in the sense that they no longer receive positive benefits; (2) some households will enroll in the program but where their units do not meet standards at enrollment they will be discouraged from expending the effort necessary to become participants; and (3) they will discourage some households from bothering to enroll. In the paragraphs below we consider the first two of these effects.

What share of households receiving housing subsidy payments in 1979 would stop receiving payments (i.e., those whose payments no longer exceeded zero) if the Reagan administration's proposals were added to the changes legislated in 1981? The percentage reductions are as follows:

Household Type	*Percentage Change*
Husband-wife family, with two children	−36%
Elderly couples	−35
Elderly individuals	−17
Other households	−20
All households combined	−21

These are major reductions. Of course, because of various "grandfathering" provisions it would take some time for these changes to occur; nevertheless they provide a reasonable measure of expected impact. Note that because of the substantially lower incomes of elderly individuals compared to elderly couples the percentage reduction for individuals is only about half of that for couples.

If program sizes are maintained, those households made ineligible by the new provisions will be replaced by other, poorer households. How are the elderly likely to fare? If past patterns hold, they may do reasonably well. The principal reason is that a greater share of the elderly pass program requirements at enrollment than do the nonelderly. Thus, as the incentives for making a special effort to qualify for payments—and such effort is required by those who do not qualify at enrollment—is reduced dramatically, fewer households will make the effort. Thus, overall enrollment patterns will be increasingly driven by the extent to which families qualify in place. Under these conditions vouchers have more of an income supplement impact and less of a housing impact (see table 6-9).

This line of argument is supported by several facts. First, we saw in table 6-6 that 24 percent of elderly enrollees in the demand experiment min-

TABLE 6-8
ESTIMATED PERCENTAGE CHANGE IN SUBSIDIES TO CURRENT HOUSING PROGRAM PARTICIPANTS FROM CHANGES ENACTED IN 1981 OR PROPOSED FOR ENACTMENT IN 1982[a]

Household Type	*Increased Participant Rent Share, .25 to .30 (1981 Law)*	*Count subsidy Value of Food Stamps (Proposed)*	*Lower FMRs (Proposed)*	*All Changes Combined*
Husband-wife, with two children[b]	−18	−5	−25	−48
Elderly couples	−19	−5	−26	−51
Elderly individuals	−15	−5	−23	−44
All households[c]	−14	−6	−22	−44

SOURCE: Tabulations of Current Population Survey data.

a. 1980 rules for the Section 8 program were applied to all renter households living in subsidized housing regardless of program to get base subsidy figure. Households included in this analysis are only those that would receive a positive subsidy payment after all changes were implemented.

b. This is the "standard household" used in the statistical models.

c. Includes other household types besides those listed earlier in the table.

imum standards program met requirements at enrollment; this compares with 18 percent of the nonelderly. A similar pattern is found in the Supply Experiment as shown below using figures for the percentage of renters in South Bend who moved from enrollment to recipient status or terminated.[16] The elderly qualified their pre-enrollment units at considerably higher rates than nonelderly households on average, especially when no repairs were required to qualify.

Beyond this is another factor, one pointed out by the analysis of the last section. The transition from enrollment to recipiency status of the elderly

TABLE 6-9
PERCENTAGE OF ENROLLEES WHO QUALIFIED FOR PAYMENT IN THEIR PREENROLLMENT DWELLING

	White households		*Black households*	
	Elderly	*All*	*Elderly*	*All*
Preenrollment unit certified	*78*	*61*	*66*	*42*
Without repair	49	37	37	21
With repair	29	24	29	21

whose units do not meet requirements at enrollment is quite insensitive to benefit levels, while the transition by their nonelderly counterparts *is* sensitive.[17] Again, the reduction in benefits will probably work to the elderly's advantage in terms of their representation among all new participants in a voucher program.

Conclusion

In closing, it is essential to try to rank how well the elderly would be served under various programmatic options. Three dimensions are relevant: the share of all households assisted who are elderly regardless of the total number of households receiving assistance, the level of benefits received by households, and the relationship between the number of assisted households and those who need assistance.

The largest share of subsidy resources goes to the elderly under the program mix in effect in 1981, a mix characterized by a substantial share of new construction projects set aside for occupancy by the elderly (or nonelderly handicapped) and the elderly competing with others for all other subsidy slots. A clearly inferior option for the elderly would be a discontinuance of the construction of specially set-aside projects and the reliance on the Section 8 Existing program as structured in 1980. Nonelderly households would compete strongly for these slots and the benefits are large enough for many to induce them to hassle with landlords or move to qualify for payments.

In between is the program proposed by the Reagan administration—a few elderly-earmarked new construction projects and a massive reduction in program benefits under the voucher program. The elderly will capture a larger share of the slots than under a no-change-in-Section 8 Existing scenario. Whether this option is good public policy depends on the needs of the elderly compared to other households. If we use eligibility defined as our metric of need, then the elderly are already well served; they constitute about 33 percent of renters eligible for assistance but 40 percent of current recipients.

The benefit levels proposed by the administration are aptly termed penurious. This may not only affect the standard of living of recipients and the composition of the recipient population but also the ability of the voucher program to achieve its objective of improving housing. With the proposed benefit level, it seems likely that the vast majority of recipients will qualify for the program in the dwellings they occupy at enrollment. Thus, the proposed plan effectively precludes significant improvement in the quality of housing occupied by those eligible for the program.

The administration's decision to fix the number of housing assistance recipients at 3.8 million seems especially unfortunate given how close we are to being able to assist all elderly renters who are income eligible to receive assistance. By the end of 1983, there will be 3.6 million households receiving rental assistance; of these 1.4 will be elderly headed. In the same year 1.9 million elderly renters will be eligible for assistance. Applying the participation rates found in the open-enrollment experimental housing voucher program, we estimate that only 200,000 to 250,000 elderly renters really remain to be served. In other words, 85 percent of those who would accept assistance are already served.

A superior option is to pursue a broad strategy of placing greater reliance on the existing stock in implementing housing policy, but to continue to expand the number of households assisted (allowing for ultimate full integration of housing assistance in the welfare system) and to keep subsidy levels higher than those proposed by the administration so that the housing upgrading objective can be accomplished. How can adequate participation of the elderly be ensured? This should not be a problem in the limited enrollment program of the foreseeable future. Simple resort to the proportionality requirements of the type found in the Housing Assistance Plans should be sufficient. Where it is not, modest outreach efforts, possibly combined with help in finding suitable units where necessary, will certainly do the trick.

Overall, a voucher program that accepts the administration's technical changes to Section 8 Existing but maintains higher benefit levels offers an effective means of helping many elderly with their housing problems while allowing them to remain in units of their own choice. However, vouchers should be used to expand the number of the poor being helped to live in good housing, not merely to maintain current participants.

NOTES

Notes to Chapter Two

1. In 1978, for example, the poverty definition for an elderly couple was only $800 higher than that for an individual ($3,947 vs. $3,159). The difference in the poverty cutoffs between a nonelderly individual and a family of three was about $1,600.

2. More specifically, the first scenario assumed that the unemployment rate would fall to 5.2 percent, inflation would fall to 4 percent, and that real labor income per worker would grow at 1.75 percent per annum. Social Security benefits would be unchanged from those in effect in 1977.

In the second scenario, the government is assumed to pursue a more vigorous growth policy. Unemployment falls to 4 percent, but inflation is at 6 percent. Growth in real labor income per worker is 2.0 percent per year. Rules for Social Security change as follows to encourage greater attachment to the labor force: (1) The reduction in benefits in retiring before age 65 was increased to 8 percent for those retiring at age 64, 16 percent at 63, and 24 percent at 62. (2) The bonus for delaying retirement past age 65 was increased to 5 percent per year beginning in 1982. (3) The benefit reduction rate applied to earnings of Social Security beneficiaries was decreased from 50 to 40 percent.

3. Details are provided in Newman, Struyk, and Manson (1982). For more information on the HUD/Simonson definition, see Simonson (1981).

4. Details are given in Struyk (1982).

5. See Struyk and Soldo (1980), pp. 68–71.

6. This point is made by Beebout, Peabody, and Doyle (1980); they particularly point out the much higher variance in electricity expenditures across income groups.

7. On these points see Golant (1972 and 1978).

8. We have used 1973 data in this case because it is the only year that the AHS figures have been seen separately tabulated for the elderly and published in a readily usable form. Lawton and his colleagues prepared the figures and they are published in U.S. Department of Housing and Urban Development (1979).

9. For further discussion of the types of housing adjustments made by the elderly when they do relocate, see Struyk (1980).

Notes to Chapter Three

1. This chapter considers elderly participation in federally supported renter assistance programs before the Reagan administration took office in 1981. Since that time, there has actually been an increase in the total number of assisted units because of commitments made prior to 1981 and because of the time lag required to get these units occupied. In the next chapter we

will discuss post-1981 estimates in more detail. Here, we rely on progress statistics from pre-Reagan years.

2. Not all of the programs that presently serve a large number of households are considered here in detail. Housing assistance, especially programs on the supply side, usually involve long-term commitments by the government. Thus, long after a program stops growing or begins to be phased out, households are still served, sometimes in large numbers. While size is one consideration, so too are data availability and the importance of the approach in current developments in housing assistance. Therefore, we analyze here those housing programs which have served large numbers of people *and* represent the primary means of housing assistance delivery in shaping pre-1981 policy

Likewise, not all of the characteristics of elderly households which are of interest are contained in any given data base. The race and sex of head, location, household composition, and income information are generally available and are documents for program participants below. As we saw in chapter 2, these factors are related to the housing circumstances of the elderly in significant ways, so it is important to know how program participants are differentiated by such characteristics. A major omission in this list is a variable designated "health status," to determine whether the elderly person is "handicapped" or "disabled." Unfortunately, there are no uniform definitions used across data bases for such variables, making program comparisons meaningless.

3. For a detailed discussion of these issues, see Struyk (1980a).

4. Calculations of the number of units assisted by Section 8 are especially complicated by the fact that in some cases, more than one form of assistance is provided. Section 8 "Loan Management" subsidies, for example, are provided for units which previously had a HUD insured loan, most often under the Section 236 program. This program is discussed later in the chapter. Paul Burke estimates that 197,000 units were assisted by both programs in 1979 (Burke, 1981, p. 5).

5. The 70 percent figure is based on counting "Loan Management" subsidies.

6. For a discussion of the various responsibilities of tenants, landlords, and the administering agency in alternative designs for existing housing programs, see Zais, Goedert, and Trutko (1979), pp. 38–45.

7. More recently, it has become possible for housing authorities that administer the public housing program to take a more direct role in Section 8 new construction and rehabilitation projects. In these cases, the authority becomes the prime sponsor, finds a developer, and provides permanent financing through its own tax-exempt bonds.

8. *Budget for Fiscal Year 1981, U.S. Department of Housing and Urban Development,* p. 4–9.

9. HUD staff estimates that this includes about 95 percent of all Section 202 projects.

10. Estimate provided by HUD staff.

11. In 1979 an estimated 86,000 units under Section 202 also received a rent supplement. The program, by itself, accounted for another 84,000 units without a Section 236 subsidy. Burke (1981), p. 5.

12. See The Institute for Research on Poverty (1977).

13. For evidence of this, see MacMillan and Hamilton (1977), pp. 25–27. The influence of outreach on the elderly in voucher-like programs is considered in more detail in chapter 6.

14. On this issue, see Goedert (1979) and the discussion in chapter 6.

15. For greater detail on family unit definitions in federal housing legislation, see Bishop, Bryson, and Calmore (1982). The primary exceptions to eligibility are single individuals who are nonelderly and neither handicapped nor disabled. With HUD approval and within a limit of 15 percent, such individuals can be assisted.

16. Struyk and Blake (1982).

17. 42 USC Section 1437d(c)(4)(A).

18. For more detail on the sampling, see Loux and Sadacca (1980).

19. For more detail on the sampling, see The Granville Corporation (1981).

20. For more detail on the sampling, see Wallace, et al. (1981).

Notes to Chapter Four

1. Public Law 97-35, August 13, 1981.
2. Khadduri (1981).
3. Newman, Struyk, and Manson (1982).
4. For more detail on the Urban Institute TRIM Model, see Thibodeau, Bergsman, and Anderson (1982).
5. Op. cit.
6. Omnibus Budget Reconciliation Act of 1981, Conference Report 97th Congress, 1st Session, p. 688.
7. Tebbets (1979) p. 17.
8. Lane (1977).
9. See Lane (1977) for various views on this issue.

Notes to Chapter Six

1. In the Section 8 Existing program the voucher is good for 60 days but can be renewed; in the experiments there was generally a 90-day time limit.
2. The general structure of this table is based on the number of eligible households estimated through a baseline survey; not all narrowly defined household groups were adequately represented in the survey to permit reliable counts of eligibles. Thus, for some groups reliable enrollment rate estimates (the ratio of enrollees to eligible households) are not available. Enrollment data are for the end of the second program year, so there is a two-year gap between the baseline eligibility figures and the enrollment figures. As a consequence, all of the figures in the table are approximations. Separate data for minorities are presented for South Bend only, because of the small number of minorities in Green Bay.
3. In particular we draw on the work of Wendt (1981).
4. For a summary of outreach efforts see Struyk and Bendick (1981), chapter 10.
5. Survey respondents were considered knowledgeable on the basis of their answers to two simple, straightforward questions. All were asked, "Have you heard about the housing allowance program which has been introduced in (site)?" If they responded yes they were then asked, "Suppose somebody asked you about the housing allowance program—how would you describe it?" The knowledge variable was then constructed by assigning a zero to respondents who admitted lack of knowledge, a one if they claimed knowledge but could furnish no details of the program, and a two if they claimed knowledge and could furnish details.

Because the enrollment model consists of two stages in which eligibles first acquire knowledge of the program and then decide to enroll, it is necessary to construct a variable that distinguishes those who knew about the program from those who did not. We assumed that those who did not know about it included those who said they did not, and that households who could give at least one valid detail of the program were very likely knowledgeable. The question remained, did those who claimed to know about the program, but were unable to provide any details, actually know about it at all?

6. Wendt classifies life-cycle as a "needs" variable.
7. Struyk and Bendick (1981), chapter 4.
8. For an overview discussion see Struyk and Bendick (1981), pp. 63–64.
9. At the end of the experimental period the Section 8 program was operated in each site. FMRs were set at virtually the same level as FMR in both instances.
10. Other criteria were that the participant had to be a renter and not be a nonelderly single individual.
11. The assignment process was not entirely random, in that extra-low income limits were set for assignment to some treatment cells. Without such a procedure, many households in these cells would have been entitled to only a small subsidy or none at all, due to their high incomes.

12. Struyk-Bendick (1981), table 4-2.

13. In the Kennedy-MacMillan formulation (1980, pp. 112–14), another term is included, the residual from a regression of enrollment housing expenditure on various household characteristics. Since the explanation for its inclusion is somewhat complex and because the term proved to be persistently insignificant in the statistical work, we do not discuss it further.

14. The models have been estimated using ordinary least squares regressions techniques. While this technique has well-known limitations when the dependent variable is dichotomous (i.e., 0, 1), these are considerably mitigated when the mean value of the dependent variable is in the 0.3 to 0.7 range as it is in this case. The coefficient estimates are unbiased, but the efficiency of the estimate is.

We have examined the frequency with which the probability of participation predicted using the estimated model falls outside of the 0, 1 interval and have found very few such cases, suggesting that quality of the estimate is reasonably good.

15. Tabulations were done using data from the Current Population Survey.

16. Figures from Struyk-Soldo (1980), table 7–11.

17. Separate multivariate analyses for the elderly and nonelderly have not been published by The Rand Corporation for the Supply Experiment.

REFERENCES

Beebout H., G. Peabody, and P. Doyle (1980), *The Distribution of Household Energy Expenditures and the Impact of High Prices*. Washington, D.C.: Paper presented at the RFF-Brookings Conferences on "High Energy Costs: The Differential Impact."

Bishop, Catherine M., David B. Bryson, and John O. Calmore (1982), "Legal Contraints Governing Public Housing Authorities' Admissions and Tenant Assignment Decisions." Berkeley, California: National Housing Law Project.

Burke, Paul (1981), "Equality in Subsidizied Housing." Washington, D.C.: U.S. Department of Housing and Urban Development.

Fein, J., and C. S. White, Jr. (1977), *The Ratio of Shelter Expenditures to Income: Definitional Issues, Typical Patterns, and Historical Trends*. Cambridge, Mass.: Abt Associates, Inc.

Goedert (1979), "Earmarking Housing Allowances: The Trade-off Between Housing Consumption and Program Participation." Washington, D.C.: The Urban Institute.

______ and L. L. Goodman, Jr. (1976), "Indicators of Housing Quality: An Exploration of the Annual Housing Survey." Washington, D.C.: The Urban Institute.

Golant, S. M. (1972), *The Residential Location and Spatial Behavior of the Elderly*. Chicago: Chemistry of Change, Department of Geography, Research Paper No. 43.

______ (1978), "Residential Contencrations of the Future Elderly," *The Gerontologist*, February, pp 19–26.

The Granville Corporation (1981), *Study of Repair and Maintenance Activity of the Section 8 Existing Housing Program: Documentation Report*. Washington, D.C.

Hoffman, W. (1979), The Distribution of Home Energy Expenditures by American Households in 1976–1977: An Analysis of Energy Need Among Low-Income Groups." Washington, D.C.: The Urban Institute.

Institute for Research on Poverty (1977), *The Treatment of Assets and Income From Assets in Income-Conditioned Government Benefit Programs*. Madison, Wisconsin: University of Wisconsin.

Kennedy, Stephen D., and Jean MacMillan (1980), *Participation Under Alternative Housing Allowance Programs: Evidence from the Housing Allowance Demand Experiment*. Cambridge, Massachusetts: Abt Associates, Inc.

Khadduri, Jill (1981), "Serving the Truly Needy." Washington, D.C.: U.S. Department of Housing and Urban Development, (draft).

Lane, Terry S. (1977), *Origins and Uses of the Conventional Rules of Thumb*. Cambridge, Massachusetts: Abt Associates, Inc.

Loux, Suzanne B., and Robert Sadacca (1980), *comparison of Public Housing Tenant Characteristics: 1976 and 1979*. Washington, D.C.: The Urban Institute.

MacMillian, Jean, and William L. Hamilton (1977), *Outreach: Generating Applications in the Administrative Agency Experiment*. Cambridge, Massachusetts: Abt Associates, Inc.

Newman, S., R. Struyk, and D. Manson (1982), "Poverty, Housing Deprivation and Housing Assistance." Washington, D.C.: The Urban Institute, Contract Report 3089–01

Newman, S., R. Struyk, and J. Zais (1982), "Housing for Older America," The Physical Environment and the Elderly, I. Altman et al., eds. (New York, N.Y.: Plenum Press).

Pitkin, J. and G. Masnick (1979), *Projection of National Housing Needs: 1980–2000*. Cambridge, Mass.: Joint Center for Urban Studies, Harvard-MIT.

Schieber, S. J. (1978), "Housing Conditions of Aged Welfare Recipients," Washington, D.C.: Social Security Administration, Unpublished.

Simonson, J. (1981), *Measuring Inadequate Housing Through Use of the Annual Housing Survey*. Washington, D.C.: U.S. Department of Housing and Urban Development, Office of Policy Development and Research.

Soldo, B. J. (1978), "Incomes of Black Aged: Their Determinants and Consequences." paper Presented at the Conference on Blacks and Retirement: An Untapped National Resource, sponsored by the Council on Minority Planning and Strategy. Washington, D.C.: Center for Population Research.

Struyk, R. (1982), *The Demand for Specially Adopted Housing by Elderly-Headed Households*. Washington, D.C.: The Urban Institute.

——— (1981), "The Changing Housing and Neighborhood Environment of the Elderly: A Look at the Year 2000." in S. B. Kiesler, J. N. Morgan, V. K. Oppenheimer (eds.), *Aging: Social Change*. New York: Academic Press.

——— (1981a), "Home Energy Costs and the Housing of the Poor and the Elderly" paper presented at the Brookings Institution Conference on Housing and Energy in the 1980s; paper to be published in a conference proceedings volume.

——— (1980), "Housing Adjustments of Relocating Elderly Households," *The Gerontologist*, vol. 20, no. 1.

——— (1980a), *A New System for Public Housing: Salvaging a National Resource*. The Urban Institute Press. Washington, D.C.

——— (1977), "The Housing Situation of Elderly Americans," *The Gerontologist* vol. 17, nos. 130–39.

Struyk, Raymond J., and Marc Bendick, Jr. editors (1981), *Housing Vouchers for the Poor: Lessons from a National Experiment*. Washington, D.C.: The Urban Institute Press.

Struyk, Raymond J., and Jennifer L. Blake (1982), *Determining Who Lives in Public Housing*. Washington, D.C.: The Urban Institute.

Struyk, Raymond J., and Beth J. Soldo (1980), *Improving the Elderly's Housing*. Cambridge, Massachusetts: Ballinger Publishing Company.

Tebbets, Paul E. (1979), *Controlling Errors in Allowance Program Administration*. Santa Monica, California: The Rand Corporation.

Thibodeau, Thomas, Anne Bergsman and Gary Anderson (1982), *Modeling Alternative Housing Voucher Programs*. Washington, D.C.: The Urban Institute.

U.S. Bureau of the Census (1970), "Revised Equivalence Scale for Estimating Incomes or Budget Costs for Family Type." 1970, Bulletin 1570–6. Washington, D.C.: U.S. Government Printing Office.

——— (1976), *Demographic Aspects of Aging and the Older Population in the United States*. Washington, D.C.: U.S. Government Printing Office, Series P–23, No 59.

——— (1979), *Annual Housing Survey 1977, Part C, Financial Characteristics of the Housing Inventory*. Washington D.C.: U.S. Government Printing Office.

——— (1981), *Annual Housing Survey 1979, Part C, Financial Characteristics of the Housing Inventory*. Washington, D.C.: U.S. Government Printing Office.

——— (1972), *Census of Housing: 1970 Metropolitan Housing Characteristics*, Final Report HC(2)–1, United States and Regions, Appendix. Washington, D.C.: U.S. Government Printing Office.

——— (1973), *Census of Housing: 1979 Subject Reports*, Final Report HC(7)–2, Housing of Senior Citizens. Washington, D.C.: U.S. Government Printing Office.

——— (1975), *Annual Housing Survey: 1973, Part A, General Characteristics for the United States and Regions*. Current Housing Reports Series H–150–73A. Washington, D.C.: U.S. Government Printing Office.

——— (1979), *Social and Economic Characterisitics of the Older Population: 1978*, Series P–23, no. 85. Washington, D.C.: U.S. Government Printing Office.

U.S.Bureau of Labor Statistics (1968), "Three Budgets for a Retired Couple in Urban Areas of the United States, 1967–68. " Bulletin 1570–2. Washington, D.C.: U.S. Government Printing Office.

U.S. Department of Housing and Urban Development (1979), *Annual Housing Survey: 1973. Housing Characteristics of Older Americans in the United States*. Washington, D.C.: U.S. Government Printing Office.

——— (1978), *Lower Income Housing Assistance Program (Section 8): Interim Findings of Evalution Research*. Washington, D.C.: Office of Policy Development and Research.

Wallace, James E., et. al. (1981), *Participation and Benefits in the Urban Section 8 Program: New Construction and Existing Housing*. Cambridge, Massachusetts: Abt Associates, Inc.

Wendt, J. C. (1981), *Why Households Apply for Housing Allowances*. Santa Monica: The Rand Corporation. Working Draft WD–1038–HUD.

Wertheimer, R. F., II, and S. R. Zedlewski (1978), *The Aging of America: A Portrait of the Elderly in 1990*. Washington, D.C.: The Urban Institute.

Wieand, K. (1978), "Analysis of Multiple Defect Indicators of Housing Quality with Data from the 1976 Annual Housing Survey." Washington, D.C.: Office of Policy Development and Research, U.S. Department of Housing and Urban Development.

Zais, James P., Jeanne E. Goedert, and John W. Trutko (1979), *Modifying Section 8: Implications from Experiments with Housing Allowances*. Washington, D.C.: The Urban Institute.

ST. JOSEPH'S COLLEGE LIBRARY
3 1960 0014235 Y

DATE DUE

OCT 19 1985			
FEB 22 1986			
MAR 8 - 1986			
MAR 22 1986			
APR 05			
JUN 2			

Do Not Remove 2/09 Date